TECHNOCRACY

THE HARD ROAD TO

WORLD ORDER

by Patrick M. Wood

"We are building the global society without a global leader. Global order is no longer something that can be dictated or controlled from the top down. Globalization itself is the order." - Dr. Parag Khanna

Printed in the United States of America

First Printing, 2018

ISBN 978-0-9863739-8-5

Coherent Publishing, LLC
P.O. Box 52247
Mesa, Arizona 85208
www.Technocracy.news

DEDICATION

This book is dedicated to the fleeting memories of Unalienable Rights, Freedom, Liberty and the Constitution of the United States. May they yet inspire future generations.

TABLE OF CONTENTS

TECHNOCRATS: A POSTMODERN PEAN

Technocrats, the story goes,
Will solve the horrid mess-
Where ethics fail, the gadgets work
And will bring about success.
Just plug it in and hit the key
And let the old brain rest;
Just what we should or should not do
Technology can answer best.

But gadgets they may be the cause
Of the Angst the people feel,
For science is cold and does not care,
About the commonweal.
Old Kant still whispers his moral laws
But few still hear his voice;
All's relative and there is no truth,
Just leave it to personal choice.

Computers buzz and wheels go 'round
And Bentham and Mill are dead;
The person's free to do his thing
Morality has all gone to bed.
All is freedom and self-esteem,
Leaving conscience as the guide,
The world is fun and is a game
With technocracy by my side.

I am the Postmodern Man,
And man means woman, too;
What is the purpose of our lives?
There's not the slightest clue.
We do our race through cyberspace
And compose the digital thunder;
Just how technology does for the soul
Causes me to wonder.

- John Calhoun Merrill (1924-2012)

ACKNOWLEDGEMENTS

There is nothing easy about writing a book, especially when it comes to editing and proofing. Things like punctuation and misspelling are relatively easy to catch, but testing concepts, wordings and contexts is much more difficult. A lot of work went into getting it just right. There were three people in particular who sifted every word, sentence and paragraph to make numerous corrections and clarifications: My eagle-eyed wife, Charmagne, friend Gail Hardaway who is a retired English professor and friend Charlene Ives who is an avid reader with a penchant for detail. Special thanks also to readers of Technocracy.News who have been my eyes and ears all over the world by forwarding articles, books, videos and other tips to me.

FOREWORD

The saying that people can't see the forest for the trees is more accurate today than ever before. They are more puzzled, bemused, frustrated, angry, and even lost because a small group of people convinced society that only they knew what to do. The individual feels he has lost control. Many books try to explain how to handle the situation, but they usually only work for a few people, specialized groups, or specific circumstances. This book, explains in a clear, simple, factually supported, but interesting and exciting way, how this developed. More important, it goes back to a pre-specialist world when there were general rules and a few exceptions. Now, everything is an exception and confusion reigns. Fortunately, this book explains everything, so it applies to everyone.

I told an American audience that Osama bin Laden said that the west had lost its moral direction. They were then shocked when I said that he is absolutely correct. I put the comment in perspective by saying that I don't want his morality either. People struggle with the challenges of today's increasingly confusing and complex world. They understand what the English poet William Wordsworth meant in his poem,

The world is too much with us; late and soon,

Getting and spending, we lay waste our powers;

Little we see in Nature that is ours;

We have given our hearts away, a sordid boon!

This Sea that bares her bosom to the moon;

The winds that will be howling at all hours,

And are up-gathered now like sleeping flowers,

For this, for everything, we are out of tune;

It moves us not. - Great God! I'd rather be

A pagan suckled in a creed outworn;

So might I, standing on this pleasant lea,

Have glimpses that would make me less forlorn;

Have sight of Proteus rising from the sea;
Or hear old Triton blow his wreathèd horn.

Wordsworth identified our challenge and the challenges of our world. He was born in 1770 at a time when the world was beginning to witness a major transformation. Science and technology offered relief away from the blood, sweat, and tears of living. However, while it offered great benefits, there was a hidden danger because it put power in the hands of very few people. I remember learning about studies in the 1960s almost inconceivable today, that located small isolated Pacific islands with no technology and introduced a metal axe. It transformed everything in ways they did not anticipate. It is a micro-example of what occurred in the world since the advent of science and technology. The group with the axe controlled everything.

Wordsworth died in 1850 just 9 years before Darwin published his seminal work *Origin of Species*. His work was profoundly different than any science before him. In fact, the word "scientist" doesn't appear until the late 19th century. Darwin was a naturalist, and that point is critical to the central theme of this book. Before Darwin, science evolved in what those technocrats with specific natural abilities arrogantly identify as its pure form. Copernicus said the Earth orbits the Sun, but proof did not appear for 275 years. Research shows at least 25% of Americans believe the pre-Copernican view. The point is it didn't matter to most people. Newton explained gravity and planetary motion, but it was of no consequence to most. However, everything changes when Darwin's theory challenges everybody. To put it provocatively, he said you and your grandmother are apes and no better than them.

Science chose Darwin and his theory to defeat religion. Before him, universities had two major faculties, the Natural Sciences and the Humanities. By effectively eliminating God as the explanation for humans being so different from all the other animals, they left a void, which was then filled by the now largest faculty on all campuses, the Social Sciences. That term is central to the theme of this book because it implies you can quantify humans and human behavior and therefore manipulate it.

Wordsworth didn't offer a solution other than to suggest we go back to a primitive, animistic state we already moved beyond. "I'd rather be a pagan suckled in a creed outworn." His problem is that before you find solutions, you must first recognize, identify, and understand the problem.

Patrick Wood does precisely that in this book. It identifies the birth, evolution, and intrusive nature of the exploitation of science and technology by a group, accurately and adequately identified as technocrats. It provides a perspective on what appear to be disparate, disconnected, events. It cuts through the forest planted by a small group and used to control individuals and collections of individuals. It allows you to step back and take the urgency out of life. It allows you to counter what H.L. Mencken described:

The whole aim of practical politics is to keep the populace alarmed, and hence clamorous to be led to safety, by menacing it with an endless series of hobgoblins, all of them imaginary.

Dr. Timothy Ball

PREFACE

I fear that they may place too implicit a confidence in their public servants, and fail properly to scrutinize their conduct; that in this way they may be made the dupes of designing men, and become the instruments of their own undoing. Make them intelligent, and they will be vigilant; give them the means of detecting the wrong, and they will apply the remedy. - Daniel Webster, 1837

In the last two years, great emphasis has been placed on "Make America Great Again". Few have considered what made America great in the first place. Any American who has traveled overseas can immediately appreciate the benefits of living in America: freedom to travel, higher income, consumer goods for every lifestyle, learning opportunities, opportunities to compete, etc. But are these really what makes America great in the first place?

Alas, no!

The foundation stones of American greatness are found in the Declaration of Independence and the U.S. Constitution. The Declaration stated,

We hold these truths to be self-evident, that all men are cre-ated equal, that they are endowed by their Creator with cer-tain unalienable Rights, that among these are Life, Liberty and the pursuit of Happiness.

The authors understood that these rights were not conferred by men, but rather by their Creator. Thus, when man attempts to take away these rights, they are not only misplaced in the order of things, but they are also setting themselves against God Himself.

The resulting form of government is called a Constitutional Republic, as opposed to a Democracy or any other form of gov-ernment. The checks and balances between the three main bodies of the Republic, Executive, Judicial and Congress, are meant to prevent runaway power of any one group.

The Constitution protects our rights to own property and to use it for our own enjoyment and economic purposes. Other countries that do not support the right to own property have always been given to mediocrity, corruption and poverty.

In the last 50 years, enemies of the Constitutional Republic and the Constitution itself have arisen to destroy both. They are haters of freedom and liberty and haters of all those who would esteem them. They are simultaneously haters of an anchored morality as found in the Ten Commandments, the Bible and philosophy in general.

Nevertheless, America is the last bastion of Freedom and Liberty in the world, and this is not lost on those who want to conquer the earth for their own pleasure and purposes. In short, America stands in their way, and they hate us for it. Like a spoiled and unreasoning toddler, they want *their way* and they want it *now!*

Many Americans are starting to wake up to these attacks but are still in a fog as to how it could have happened in the first place. More are searching for what they can do to overcome these would-be usurpers. Others are discouraged and ready to give up entirely.

This book seeks to address all of these issues. I have tried my best to take complex issues and make them easy to understand and in a compact form. There is a risk that I have said too little on certain topics and perhaps too much on others, but I expect it will balance out to give you a good understanding of the state of the world in a relatively short period of time. My overriding desire is that you will be better equipped to find lasting and effective solutions.

Patrick M. Wood
Author

INTRODUCTION

It will look like a great "booming, buzzing confusion,"
but an end-run around national sovereignty, eroding it
piece by piece, will accomplish much more than the old-
fashioned frontal assault. - Richard Gardner [2]

Few people would confess that the modern world makes any sense. National governments are dysfunctional. Economic activity defies traditional analysis. Debt levels are simply inconceivable. There is no diplomacy or civility left anywhere in the world. Violence and barbarity are not just limited to Islamic terrorists, but now include radicals, malcontents and snapped individuals from all walks of life.

The Trilateral Commission was co-founded by David Rockefeller and Zbigniew Brzezinski in 1973 with the stated purpose of creating a *New International Economic Order* (NIEO). Subsequently, elite members from North America, Europe and Japan gave birth to modern globalization and have literally transformed the entire global economic structure.

To readers of this book, the societal outcomes above will soon be seen as the natural outcomes and consequences of the Trilateral Commission imposing Technocracy on the world through its NIEO. This author was an eye-witness in those early days, with able scholarship from the late Professor Antony C. Sutton, and together we had many direct interactions and debates with Commission members.

In 1974, original Trilateral Commission member and academ-

---

2 *Foreign Affairs*, Vol. 52, Number 3, 1974, pp 557-576..

ic Richard Gardner wrote a seminal paper that was published in *Foreign Affairs*, the official publication of the Council on Foreign Relations. Obsessed with the Trilateral goal of creating a "New International Economic Order", Gardner titled his article, *The Hard Road To World Order*.[3]

Gardner had the French Revolution on his mind, as he bracketed his thoughts with quotes from Charles Dickens' famous literary classic, *A Tale of Two Cities*:

> *It was the best of times, it was the worst of times, it was the age of wisdom, it was the age of foolishness, it was the epoch of belief, it was the epoch of incredulity, it was the season of Light, it was the season of Darkness, it was the spring of hope, it was the winter of despair, we had everything before us, we had nothing before us, we were all going direct to Heaven, we were all going direct the other way.*

Nothing about the French Revolution was uplifting or inspiring. In fact, it was one of the bloodiest and most irrational assaults on humankind in history. The wanton killing, executions, chaos and societal darkness persisted from 1789 to 1799 and ultimately led to the tyrannical dictatorship of Emperor Napoleon Bonaparte. Indeed, Napoleon changed the world forever, presaging the rise of global socialism, communism and revolution.

Gardner's oft-repeated statement that followed gives us an insight into his radical idea to turn the world upside-down:

> *In short, the "house of world order" will have to be built from the bottom up rather than from the top down. It will look like a great "booming, buzzing confusion," but an end-run around national sovereignty, eroding it piece by piece, will accomplish much more than the old-fashioned frontal assault.*[4]

We should not miss the point that the French Revolution followed the same pattern, that is, from the 'bottom up". Although Gardner was not recommending bloodshed, as was the case in France, he did foresee the existing world order succumbing to a

3 *Foreign Affairs*, Vol. 52, Number 3, 1974, pp 557-576.

4 Ibid.

process figuratively similar to the barbaric Chinese practice of "death by a thousand cuts".

Since 1974, the systematic dismantling of national, state and personal sovereignty, the reformation of global trade and the ad hominem attacks on those critical of their "plan" have all served to create the "booming, buzzing confusion" that we experience today.

In this, Gardner was right: It is going to be a *very hard road*.

In the conclusion to *Technocracy Rising: The Trojan Horse of Global Transformation*, I wrote,

> *If today's technocrats are meticulously working toward a scientific dictatorship and applying a specific strategy to get there, wouldn't you think that they have a specific list of criteria that must be met before "game over" can be called?*

With the rapid advances in Smart City technology, mass surveillance, the Internet of Things, 5G rollouts and now massive censorship of all opposing positions, it seems that "game over" may have actually already been called; if not, it is certainly very close.

China is now widely acknowledged (in academic circles, at least) as having transitioned to a full-blown Technocracy. It has the outward trappings of Communism left over from the last century, but it has now superseded Marxism and Communism, and has promoted it to other nations around the world.

The China transformation was aptly predicted by Trilateral Commission co-founder Zbigniew Brzezinski in his 1970 book, *Between Two Ages: America's Role in the Technetronic Era*. He maintained that Marxism, Communism and Socialism were merely the necessary stepping-stones to reach his "Technetronic Era" but were not themselves the intended endgame. I consider Brzezinski to be venerated on this point.

A book was released by Dr. Parag Khanna in 2015 titled, *Technocracy in America*, issues a blunt call to implement a direct Technocracy in the U.S. He calls for the abolishment of the Senate, the replacement of the Executive office by a committee of co-

Presidents and the surrender of the Constitution to the Supreme Court for modernization.

Big Tech has since become the engine of mass censorship of non-complying thought, most of which is conservative. Twitter, YouTube, Google, Facebook and even Amazon have seemingly colluded to exclude "deniers" from their respective platforms. Credit card processors like Stripe, Mastercard and Paypal have joined them to summarily cut off funding from conservative websites and organizations.

The new telecom standard, 5G, is stampeding into cities around the world with such blinding speed that there is hardly time to mount a protest. Leaders of the 5G revolution like AT&T and Verizon, have bluntly and openly stated that 5G is not about SmartPhones but rather about enabling the Internet of Things and all other Smart City technologies.

Mass surveillance technology has exploded around the world with facial-recognition cameras, sensors, artificial intelligence and analytics. China expects to have 600 million facial recognition cameras installed by 2020. In Chinese cities that are already blanketed with these cameras, any person can be located and collared within minutes of putting out the command to do so.

Public-Private Partnerships, a creation of the UN's Sustainable Development policies, are blanketing the U.S. under the leadership of President Donald Trump. For every taxpayer dollar spent on public projects and especially on infrastructure, there will be up to $10 of corporate money spent.

It should be clear that the march toward Technocracy is neither Democrat or Republican, liberal or conservative, Marxist or Capitalist. Since 1973, every Administration has promoted it and followers of every ideology have served as its "useful idiots."

Some of these things are certainly recognized more readily than others. The main thought is, the point of inflection to establish full-blown Technocracy is much closer today than ever before. This book will extend the work of *Technocracy Rising* to flesh out the demise of nationalism and the rise of global cities, the global supply chain and Scientific Dictatorship.

Thus, without apology or hesitation, I dedicate this book in protest to Professor Richard Newton Gardner who was first to tell us about the "Hard Road" we have experienced since 1974.

Booming, buzzing confusion, indeed.

Chapter 1

The Basics of Technocracy

The scientists have the future in their bones.
                                        - C.P. Snow
        No, they don't.
            - P.M. Wood

By 1932, America had fallen into deep economic depression. During the three years since the precipitous stock market crash of 1929, ten thousand banks failed, the economy shrank by thirty-one percent, international trade fell by two-thirds and unemployment rose to almost twenty-four percent.

It should not be surprising that many Americans believed that their national economic system was mortally wounded. Politicians and bankers were widely believed to be responsible: the politicians as corrupt and bumbling fools and the bankers as malevolent, vampire squids. Unfortunately, people also realized how helpless they were to change anything, and this drained whatever hope was left.

At the same time, the media giant Randolph Hearst was trying to hang on to his flagship, Hearst Communications that owned no fewer than 30 major newspapers in the largest American cities and many national magazines. At its peak, Hearst Communications was the largest media company in the world. Nevertheless, Hearst was fighting for his very existence by 1932, trying every trick in a publisher's playbook to hold on to readership and advertising revenue.

By the early 1930s, Hearst had already developed a reputation for so-called yellow journalism, having "routinely invented sensational stories, faked interviews, run phony pictures and distorted real events."[8] With the whole world already largely detached from reality, most readers couldn't recognize fake news or wouldn't care if they did. That news might also be corrupted only fit in with the larger picture of political corruption, anger and despair.

The stage is now set to introduce Nicholas Murray Butler, President of Columbia University in New York. Although both of them were national figures, there was no love lost between Hearst and Butler who had been attacked by Hearst as an "arch-propagandist for un-American principles".[9] Indeed, Butler was the paragon of progressivism in America while Hearst was just as passionately anti-Communist and anti-Fascist.

Nevertheless, Hearst smelled a big story when Butler announced in early fall 1932 that Columbia University was backing a brand new economic system being designed by scientists and engineers that could replace Capitalism and Free Enterprise and quite literally rescue the whole world. Since politicians and economists had already failed, why not give the scientists and engineers a shot at it? Even more compelling was the name of this new economic system: *Technocracy*.

Well, this *was* news and the Hearst syndicate wasted no time in jumping on it. Here was a unique story of something truly new that could restore hope to a hopelessly lost and dying economic system. And most importantly, delivering a hopeful message would certainly build readership and, in fact, it *did*! The presses ran hot all over America, cranking out story after story on the coming miracle age of the scientific society, if only the scientists and engineers could work out all the details. Many Americans

---

8 Martin Lee, and Martin Solomon, *Unreliable Sources: A Guide to Detecting Bias in News Media*, (L Trade Paper, 1991).

9 Ben Proctor, *William Randolph Hearst: The Later Years, 1911-1951*, (Oxford University Press, 2007), p. 197.

swooned, cheered and then bought even more newspapers and magazines to stay up with the latest developments.

While it was true that Hearst had lowered his principles to support anything coming out of Columbia University, his concerns might have been assuaged when he discovered that the Technocrats, those scientific and engineering saviors, were also pointedly anti-Communist. In fact, an implicit side-benefit of Technocracy would be to permanently erase Communism from America which undoubtedly helped Hearst's decision to get behind it.

Throughout the fall and winter of 1932, Hearst and Butler were seemingly on the same page. However, neither of them realized that they were being conned by the messianic leader of the Technocracy group, Howard Scott. Scott relished the attention he received at Columbia, and he loved to give interviews to any reporter who would listen, most of whom were employed by Hearst newspapers. The bubble suddenly popped when it was discovered that Scott did not have the engineering degree that he claimed to have; in other words, he had pointedly defrauded both Butler and Hearst and to say that they were both livid is an understatement.

Damage control was immediate. Reputation-sensitive Butler, who had put Columbia up to be the laughing stock of global academia, summarily drop-kicked the entire Technocracy group off the Columbia campus. Hearst was no less dramatic, for the purveyor of fake news had been caught at his own game. The guillotine fell swiftly on every Hearst publication in America: Don't ever mention the word "Technocracy" again or you will be fired. Not surprisingly, no more stories on Technocracy appeared in Hearst publications.

This could have been the end of Technocracy, but it wasn't. Howard Scott's ego was bigger than rejections from Butler or Hearst. Even though he was dead broke by spring of 1933, he maintained a friendship with one of the earlier Technocracy crowd, M. King Hubbert. In fact, Hubbert was generous enough to take Scott in as a roommate where they continued to discuss ways to get Technocracy into the mainstream of American thought. Both were further encouraged by people around the country who had already attached themselves to the Technocracy dream.

Finally, in early 1934, Scott and Hubbert filed articles of incorporation for *Technocracy, Inc.* in New York state and created a membership organization that would require annual dues to provide operating funds. From this time forward, Technocracy as an economic ideology was fleshed out by Technocracy, Inc., and mostly by M. King Hubbert.

The *Technocracy Study Course* was published before the end of 1934 and immediately became the touchstone for everything that followed. This 291-page volume was the master architectural document that not only defined Technocracy but also presented details on how to implement it. It was grandiose in scope:

> *Technocracy is dealing with social phenomena in the widest sense of the word; this includes not only actions of human beings, but also everything which directly or indirectly affects their actions. Consequently, the studies of Technocracy embrace practically the whole field of science and industry. Biology, climate, natural resources, and industrial equipment all enter into the social picture....*[10]

Here we can make the first major observation about Technocracy; society and science are pictured as one, or at least intricately interwoven. This theme has been presented consistently and methodically at every Technocracy meeting throughout North America ever since. In 1938, their official magazine, *The Technocrat,* offered the same core belief with some additional clarification:

> *Technocracy is the science of social engineering, the scientific operation of the entire social mechanism to produce and distribute goods and services to the entire population...* [11]

Not only did they invent the "science of social engineering", but they intended to impose its methodology on the entire society. Furthermore, the object of the exercise was to produce goods

---

10 Scott and Hubbert, *Technocracy Study Course*, (Technocracy, Inc., 1934), p. ix.

11 "What is Technocracy", *The Technocrat Magazine*, 1930.

and services to everyone. There is no doubt that Technocrats themselves openly declared that Technocracy was a replacement economic system for Capitalism, and the rest of the Technocracy Study Course explained how it must be implemented and then operated by Technocrats consisting of engineers, scientists and technicians.

What commended these Technocrats to think that they were able to run society better than anyone else or, for that matter, that society would allow them to do so? Herein we find the second major observation, and it relates to Technocrats themselves: They are an egotistical bunch who have been infected by the ideological poison of Scientism. This is a fine point but one that needs to be understood because it is so very relevant to today's world as well. Early-on in the Study Course, we see the following statement:

Science is, in a dynamic sense, essentially a method of prediction. It has been defined as being the method of the determination of the most probable.[12]

This is a false narrative, but here is where it first originated: The acknowledged philosophical father of both Technocracy and Scientism was Henri de Saint-Simon (1760-1825), who wrote over one-hundred years earlier,

A scientist, my dear friends, is a man who foresees; it is because science provides the means to predict that it is useful, and the scientists are superior to all other men.[13]

"A method of prediction" and "science provides the means to predict" are fundamentally identical. They are broad sweeping statements that can only be understood through the eyes of Saint-Simon himself who went on to say that "scientists are superior to all other men." Thus, this mental superiority complex is exactly where the *real* trouble with Technocracy began.

First, Technocrats believed that every problem in society could be answered by science and only science. Second, they believed

---

12 Ibid. p. 12.
13 Letters from an Inhabitant of Geneva to His Contemporaries, (1803). *The Political Thought of Saint-Simon* (Oxford University Press, 1976).

only they and they alone could devise those answers using the same Scientific Method used in the hard sciences. Third, they believed that they and they alone must be the ones who actually run society. When I say they "believed", the proof of this lies in the fact that they consistently assumed the world would naturally bow to them and automatically turn everything over to them. Let me demonstrate.

The geographic focus of early Technocracy was exclusively on what they called the North American Technate. Their official map included Greenland, all of Canada, Alaska, the continental United States, Mexico, Cuba, all of Central America and the few northernmost countries of South America. It was assumed that somehow this entire geographic region would adopt Technocracy as its economic system and allow the scientists and engineers to control the whole thing. What is totally missing from all of their literature, and I have searched thoroughly, is any explanation or rationale on how to convince these sovereign nations to roll over into Technocracy; it just never occurred to the Technocrats that anyone would resist them. In other words, if science is fact, and facts have the last word, then who would have anything else to say?

This is the same siren call of Scientism that persists to this very day, and we see these same attitudes in all the modern aspects of Technocracy, such as Sustainable Development, Agenda 21, 2030 Agenda, Biodiversity, Global Warming, alternative energy, etc. In every case, the "science" is presented as "settled" with the implicit assumption that nobody has a reason to dispute either the science or the remedial actions that are specified to fix some perceived problem.

To a hammer, everything looks like a nail. To a Technocrat scientist or engineer, everything looks like a problem begging for a scientific or engineering solution.

It is important to make a distinction between real scientists and engineers versus their Technocrat counterparts. The latter have been infected with some degree of Scientism while the former have not. The world is full of legitimate scientists and engineers who just want to practice their craft and be otherwise left alone. They contribute greatly to the service of mankind. They have no desire to run the world or tell everyone else what they must or must not do. They are not into falsifying or misusing data to fit unprovable theories, and most of all, they are not interested in using their technologies to control people. To these, we salute!

The Technocracy Architecture

Technocracy is a resource-based economic system that uses energy as its accounting system. This is in contrast to our current economic system which is price-based (i.e., supply and demand) and uses money as its accounting system.

In a resource-based economic system, all resource inputs required for human subsistence would be carefully measured and meted out in the most efficient manner in order to eliminate wastage. All consumption would be automatically limited by issuing to all citizens a quota of energy certificates. These certificates could be spent on goods and services priced according to the energy that it took to make them in the first place. This, they reasoned, would create a Utopia-like society where people would only work 20 hours per week and yet still have abundance of material goods available for consumption.

Extensive details of the mechanics, details and rationale of Technocracy can be found in the *Technocracy Study Course* and in this author's book, *Technocracy Rising: The Trojan Horse of Global Transformation*.[14] In the interest of space, I will list a few of the more salient features in this section.

The official requirements for Technocracy are seen on page 232 of the *Study Course* and were considered necessary for normal operation of the Technate:

1. *Register on a continuous 24 hour-per-day basis the total net conversion of energy.*

2. *By means of the registration of energy converted and consumed, make possible a balanced load.*

14 Wood, Technocracy Rising: The Trojan Horse of Global Transformation, (Coherent Publishing, 2015),

3. *Provide a continuous inventory of all production and consumption.*

4. *Provide a specific registration of the type, kind, etc., of all goods and services, where produced and where used.*

5. *Provide specific registration of the consumption of each individual, plus a record and description of the individual.*

6. *Allow the citizen the widest latitude of choice in consuming his individual share of Continental physical wealth.*

7. *Distribute goods and services to every member of the population.*[15]

In items 1 and 2, you can see the focus on control over energy distribution and consumption. Items 3-5 cover the extensive collection of data that would be used to monitor and control the societal machinery. Item 6 indicates that citizens could buy anything they wanted, limited only by the number of Energy Certificates that were issued at the beginning of the accounting period. Item 7 points out that every single member of society would be in the system, with no possibility of holdouts.

Other key points to the original definition of Technocracy include,

- Private property would be eradicated altogether. Everything would be owned in common by the Technate and controlled by them.

- All price-based currencies would be abolished and replaced by a system of Energy Certificates.

- Energy Certificates would be issued at the start of an accounting period, and expired at the end of it, preventing accumulation of savings for future needs.

- All conceivable human needs (food, housing, transportation, medical, retirement, etc.) would be met by the Technate at their sole discretion.

- Traditional systems of government would be abolished, including Congress and state governments.

- A continental board of Technocrats would manage all economic and societal affairs according to Functional and Service Sequences, defined by and run by themselves.

---

15 Ibid., p. 232-233.

- Education would be transformed into human conditioning to prepare students for a lifetime of work chosen for them by the Technate.

- Science and the Scientific Method would be the sole guide to decision-making throughout the Technate, based on collected data.

Because private ownership of any resource was deemed wasteful and inefficient, Technocracy specified that all automobiles would be converted into public assets. Ride-sharing would become the new norm:

> *This would be accomplished by instituting what would resemble a national 'drive it yourself' system. The Automotive Branch of Transportation would provide a network of garages at convenient places all over the country from which automobiles could be had at any hour of the night or day. No automobiles would be privately owned. When one wished to use an automobile he would merely call at the garage, present his driver's license, and a car of the type needed would be assigned to him. 'When he was through with the car he would return it either to the same garage, or to any other garage that happened to be convenient, and surrender his Energy Certificates in payment for the cost incurred while he was using it.[16]*

If you have any understanding of modern initiatives like Agenda 21, Sustainable Development, 2030 Agenda, Global Warming, etc., you should immediately see some striking parallels to historic Technocracy. Don't be tempted to write it off as coincidental because it is not!

In all of its original self-conceived glory, Technocracy is alive and well today. But don't let anyone suggest to you that it is a modern idea cooked up by the United Nations, NGOs, economic planners or even the Trilateral Commission. It was not!

One of the keenest insights into Technocracy was offered by Aldous Huxley in 1932, at the exact same time that Nicholas Murray Butler and Randolph Hearst were crowing about the eco-

---

16 Ibid., p. 253-254.

nomic miracle being conceived at Columbia University. Huxley didn't have to look twice to see that the outcome of Technocracy would be Scientific Dictatorship. The title of his book? *Brave New World*!

CHAPTER 2

TECHNOCRACY IS SUSTAINABLE DEVELOPMENT

*America has more than enough democracy. What it
needs is more technocracy - a lot more.* - *Parag Khanna*

To establish relevance for the reader, it is necessary to demonstrate that Sustainable Development is Technocracy,
and vice versa. Even though this will make some parts of this
book redundant, it is better to cut to the chase and lay out the
case in plain and clear terms.

Since Chapter 1 has already provided some background for
understanding Technocracy, a brief explanation on the essence of
Sustainable Development will help to clarify my assertion.

The term was first coined in 1980 by the United Nations'
International Union for Conservation of Nature and Natural
Resources (IUCN) in a document called *World Conservation
Strategy*.[15] Its meaning was simply conservation that balanced
nature with economic development. The opening sentence of the
text states,

> *The aim of the World Conservation Strategy is to help ad-
> vance the achievement of sustainable development through
> the conservation of living resources.* [16]

15 World Conservation Strategy: Living Resource Conservation for Sustainable Development, World
Conservation Strategy. URL: http://data.iucn.org/dbtw-wpd/edocs/WCS-004.pdf, (1980).
16 Ibid., p. iv.

It is important to note that the term is in lowercase, indicating that it was not yet considered a proper noun. In every instance in this document it referred to economic development which they claimed was on a collision course with depleted resources unless conservation measures were put in place to balance the two. This was clearly seen in a statement like,

> For if the object of development is to provide for social and economic welfare, the object of conservation is to ensure Earth's capacity to sustain development and to support all life. [17]

Three years later in 1983, the United Nations convened the World Commission On Environment and Development (WCED) and appointed Gro Harlem Brundtland as the chairperson. Brundtland was formerly Prime Minister of Norway but had a strong background in environmental issues. She was also a member of the Trilateral Commission, which, as you will remember, was exclusively dedicated to creating a *New International Economic Order*. As the Brundtland Commission was terminated in 1987, it celebrated the publication of its outcome book, *Our Common Future*, which in 1992 became the cornerstone document in the creation of Agenda 21 policies at the first Earth Summit held in Rio de Janeiro. The Rio event was officially called the *United Nations Conference On Environment and Development* (UNCED).

The very succinct definition of Sustainable Development found in *Our Common Future* has been endlessly quoted in UN, NGO, academic and governmental literature throughout the world ever since its publication in 1987:

> Sustainable development is development that meets the needs of the present without compromising the ability of future generations to meet their own needs.[18]

While this may sound noble, the details are problematic, as seen in statements like this:

---

17 Ibid., Foreword
18 World Commission on Environment and Development, *Our Common Future*, (Oxford, 1987) p. 43

In essence, sustainable development is a process of change in which the exploitation of resources, the direction of investments, the orientation of technological development, and institutional change are all in harmony and enhance both current and future potential to meet human needs and aspirations.[19]

First, the "process of change" is all-encompassing, focusing on resources, investments, technology and governments. When viewed through the eyes of Trilateral Commission policies, which Brundtland clearly represented, one sees a plan to completely recast global economic development.

Second, "resources" are the key concern. Of course, resources are a necessary ingredient to the production of all goods and services. The problem is that those resources tied up in personal property or in poverty-stricken nations are not available to the elite global corporations. Thus, sustainable development promoted a process to free up resources for global development. This would increase the size of the economic pie as well as their share of it.

Third, "investments" must be redirected in order to take control of resources and future development. However, who controls these investments in the first place? The problem here is that the consumer-based economy was continually bumping up against growth limitations and could not satisfy the global oligarchy's desire to expand further. Public treasuries and pension funds represented by cities and governments, continually replenished by the taxation of citizens, represented a bottomless pit of investment funds. This naturally gave rise to the concept of Public-Private Partnerships (P3) where corporations and governments partner on grandiose projects to supposedly stimulate economic development. P3 has taken hold in every nation on earth and has effectively overcome the problem of springing funds from government lockup into the hands of corporate developers.

Fourth, the plan saw the need to reorient technology development toward this economic development concept. Previously,

---

19 Ibid., p. 46.

most spending on technology was focused on legitimate human needs. Today, most spending on technology is focused on sustainable development and related areas such as global warming, geo-engineering, connectivity, etc.

Last, Sustainable Development calls for changes in the institutions that govern society. The problem is that existing government structures were resistant to the exploitation proposed by sustainable development. In America, this gave rise to the Clinton and Gore initiative called the *National Partnership for Reinventing Government* (NPR). NPR was created by President Clinton's Executive Order 12862 on March 3, 1993, just one year after Agenda 21 was created by the Earth Summit in Rio in 1992. Other similar initiatives around the world have radically changed how governments view sustainable development. This also created the right environment for P3s to flourish.

In short, sustainable development promised the Utopia of eliminating poverty, providing jobs and education for all, and protecting the environment all at the same time. Indeed, these were the sales hooks used to secure buy-in to Sustainable Development in the first place.

Was Sustainable Development disingenuous or was it for real?

Pratap Chatterjee and Matthias Finger, authors of *The Earth Brokers* in 1994, were direct participants in the UN meetings leading up to the Earth Summit held in Rio in 1992. They were environmentalists of the original order that preceded globalization, and they were deeply disappointed in the entire process and outcome. They concluded that "as a result of the whole UNCED[20] process, the planet was going to be worse off, not better."[21] In further opposition, they wrote,

We argue that UNCED has boosted precisely the type of industrial development that is destructive for the environment, the planet, and its inhabitants. We see how, as a result of UNCED,

---

20 UNCED - United Nations Conference on Environment and Development. UNCED was the organizer and host of the Earth Summit held in Rio in 1992.
21 Chatterjee & Finger, *The Earth Brokers*, (Routledge, 1994), p. 2.

the rich will get richer, the poor poorer, while more and more of the planet is destroyed in the process.[22]

Such early warnings from prominent UN insiders were either marginalized or totally ignored. There is no doubt that certain elements of the environment were under stress in 1992, but it was caused by the very globalization policies created by the Trilateral Commission and its members in the first place. However, Free Trade and industrial development were never put on the table as culprits. Instead, *people* were blamed for environmental destruction. Those countries with high levels of poverty were held up as the principal culprits.

To solve these problems, a member of the Trilateral Commission, Gro Harlem Brundtland, proposed a solution that required even more development. Increased efficiency, more technological solutions and centralized control over resources would somehow make it everything better. Of course, this was nonsense. You don't tell a drug addict that his remedy to kick the habit is to get a purer form of heroin.

Toward the end of the Earth Summit, youth representatives were allowed to give their impressions of the process and proceedings, and they selected a young lady from Kenya, Wagaki Mwangi, who worked for the International Youth Environment and Development Network in Nairobi. Her short, pointed and shocking statement left many attendees in dead silence:

The Summit has attempted to involve otherwise powerless people of society in the process. But by observing the process we now know how undemocratic and untransparent the UN system is. Those of us who have watched the process have said that UNCED has failed. As youth we beg to differ. Multinational corporations, the United States, Japan, the World Bank, The International Monetary Fund have got away with what they always wanted, carving out a better and more comfortable future for themselves... UNCED has ensured increased domination by those who already have power. Worse still it has robbed the poor of the little power they

---

22 Ibid., p. 3.

had. It has made them victims of a market economy that has thus far threatened our planet. Amidst elaborate cocktails, travailing and partying, few negotiators realized how critical their decisions are to our generation. By failing to address such fundamental issues as militarism, regulation of transnational corporations, democratisation of the international aid agencies and inequitable terms of trade, my generation has been damned.[23]

While this may seem to be a harsh assessment to some readers, I am only setting up to ask this question: *If Sustainable Development is not really about saving the planet, then what is it?*

In short, it is Technocracy merely warmed over from the 1930s. Perhaps it could be called neo-Technocracy, but we will stick with Technocracy. First, here are some differences between Technocracy in 1934 and Sustainable Development in 1992 and onward.

Technocracy vs. Sustainable Development

Financial backing: The original Technocracy movement that started at Columbia University was disgraced in 1932 and had absolutely no institutional support thereafter. Operating funds were raised with membership dues. When David Rockefeller entered the scene in 1973 with the formation of the Trilateral Commission, Technocracy found its day in the sun, after which untold amounts of money poured in.

Representation: Politicians, bankers and corporatists were not allowed into early Technocracy; Technocrats believed Technocracy would ascend on its own, without any outside help when Capitalism was completely dead. The Rockefeller group understood that Technocracy could not ever take hold until these groups were actually driving it through the transitionary period. However, note that as Technocracy proceeds to gain traction today, these same groups are increasingly appearing to be the so-

---

23 Ibid., p. 167. (Note: The full text is reprinted in Third World Resurgence, 1992, No. 24/25, p. 27.)

called 'useful idiots' of Technocracy, played like violins as they promote the very system that will bury them in the end.

Scope of operations: As already noted, early Technocracy was focused on the North American continent plus part of South America. Today, Sustainable Development envelops the entire planet. This is intuitive considering that the Trilateral Commission intended to build a "New International Economic Order."

The positive identifiers between Technocracy and Sustainable Development are many and varied. Here are a few that stand out clearly.

Energy Currency: Both systems are obsessed with control over energy production and consumption. Early Technocracy wanted to replace money with Energy Certificates which it viewed as the only logical accounting system for a resource-based economy. Sustainable Development is obsessed with Carbon Credits (derived from energy), Cap and Trade programs and the uniform transfer of energy to all parts of the planet. In 2012, the International Social Transformation Conference met in Split, Croatia, and was attended by prominent economists from around the world. The theme of the conference was Energy Currency and the subtitle was "Energy as the Fundamental Measure of Price, Cost and Value."[24] Presenter topics unquestionably tied Energy Currency to Sustainable Development: *"A Better Kind of Backing: Helping Sustainable Currencies to Scale"*, *"Sustainable Money for a Sustainable Economy"* and *"Money, Energy and Sustainability"*.

Control over energy: The first two requirements of Technocracy concerned the control of energy. The second requirement stated, "By means of the registration of energy converted and consumed, make possible a balanced load."[25] This is identical to Sustainable Development's goal of renewable energy and the global smart grid; everything must be finitely controlled down to the last milliwatt.

Data-Driven: Early Technocracy proposed to collect all economic and personal data on all processes and people in society.

---

24 See website, www.teslaconference.com.
25 Op. Cit., p. 232.

The fifth requirement of the Study Course stated, "Provide specific registration of the consumption of each individual, plus a record and description of the individual."[26] Modern Sustainable Development shares the exact same obsession, where all decisions will be "data-driven" according to the scientific method. Data is viewed as causative, as one industry website states: "Big data is what will drive smart cities. It will be the force that ensures they become a reality."[27] Every agency of the United Nations is served by the UN Statistical Division (UNSD) that provides technical help to all other agencies, as well as mountains of data collected by itself.[28]

Resource-based: Early Technocracy states, "There must likewise be continuous analysis of data and resources pertaining to the Continent as a whole, both for the purposes of coordinating current and of determining long-time policies as regards probable growth curves in conjunction with resource limitation and the like."[29] The Technocracy, Inc. logo was the Chinese Monad, or Yin Yang symbol that depicted "balance" between production and consumption. Sustainable Development is obsessed with and depends on control over resources, conservation, and preservation. One definition states that it is "the organizing principle for meeting human development goals while at the same time sustaining the ability of natural systems to provide the natural resources and ecosystem services upon which the economy and society depends."[30]

Management: Early Technocracy would be managed exclusively by engineers, scientists and technicians. Original Technocrats proclaimed that "it will be the function of its engineers and technologists to put into operation a permanent productive and distributive system which will harness the energy-resources of the country for the mutual benefit of the entire population."[31] Recently, a scholar and advocate of both Sustainable Development

---

26 Op. Cit., p. 232.
27 *Making smart cities a reality: How to handle big data*, ITProPortal.com website.
28 See the www.unstats.un.org web site
29 Op. Cit., p. 227.
30 See Wikipedia, "Sustainable Development".
31 "A Statement by Technocracy", p. 1.

and Technocracy stated, "With a science PhD and a no-nonsense attitude, Germany's Angela Merkel is Europe's parliamentary technocrat par excellence."[32] He further stated, "Technocrats can make big, unpopular and painful decisions that are also urgent, necessary and even essential for national wellbeing [sic]."[33] What is a Technocrat? According to Webster, it is "a technical expert, especially on exercising managerial authority", and it notes that the first use of the word was in 1932! This attitude of elevating scientists, engineers and technicians is widespread throughout the United Nations and the Sustainable Development communities.

A final thought involves Ms. Christiana Figueres, who at the time was Executive Secretary of the United Nations Framework Convention on Climate Change (UNFCC). On February 3, 2015, Figueres addressed a press conference in Brussels, Belgium. Remembering that Climate Change is at the heart of Sustainable Development, Figures' statement was shocking, yet perfectly clear:

This is probably the most difficult task we have ever given ourselves, which is to intentionally transform the economic development model, for the first time in human history. This is the first time in the history of mankind that we are setting ourselves the task of intentionally, within a defined period of time to change the economic model that has been reigning for at least 150 years, since the industrial revolution. That will not happen overnight and it will not happen at a single conference on climate change, be it COP 15, 21, 40 - you choose the number. It just does not occur like that. It is a process, because of the depth of the transformation.[34]

Two things can be certain about this. First, Capitalism and Free Enterprise are on the chopping block, and second, Sustainable Development is the chosen replacement. Figueres herself testifies that when this happens, it will be the first occurrence of such a change in the history of the world.

---

32 Parag Khanna, Technocracy in America: The Rise of the Info State, (Createspace, 2017), p. 89.
33 Ibid., p. 106.
34 Figueres: First time the world economy is transformed intentionally, United Nations Regional Information Centre For Western Europe, Press release, February 3, 2015.

After an exhaustive historical inquiry, I can confidently state that the only specifically-designed replacement economic model created in the history of the world was: *Technocracy!*

Thus, it is clear that Sustainable Development is Technocracy and vice versa.

Making this connection now will help the reader to understand the balance of this book in its proper context. The Sustainable Development movement has taken careful steps to conceal its true identity, strategy and purpose, but once the veil is lifted, you will never see it any other way. Once its strategy is unmasked, everything else will start to make sense.

CHAPTER 3

THE UN'S PLANETARY TROIKA

The implementation of the New Urban Agenda
contributes to the implementation and localization
of the 2030 Agenda for Sustainable Development in
an integrated manner, and to the achievement of the
Sustainable Development Goals and targets[52]. - UN

Understanding that Sustainable Development is not about the environment but rather about economic development puts the entire United Nations' agenda in a different light. Whatever genuine sentiment that might have existed about stewardship of the planet forty years ago, it was mercilessly hijacked by the same people who were the root of the problem in the first place. In fact, they had no regard for nature *or* people. As discussed in the previous chapter, this hijacking was accomplished by a very narrow and focused group of internationalists as represented by members of the Trilateral Commission. The United Nations became, in effect, a proxy for this group and the universal driving force to implement its policies.

As noted by Chatterjee and Finger in 1994, the Earth Summit that produced Agenda 21 was about "more growth, more trade, more aid, more science, more technology and more management."[53] They finally concluded,

---

52 United Nations, New Urban Agenda, 2017.
53 Op Cit., p. 61.

UNCED has shown us the global horizon, but by analyzing the UNCED process we now know that the word 'global' is a mirage. It turns out to be the illusion created by the traditional agents and major stakeholders in order to maintain their privileges and to avoid questioning the fact that their traditional problem-solving mechanisms are basically bankrupt.[54]

This observation is just as valid today as it was then. However, Agenda 21 was just the kickstart to what has become a global tsunami of transformational change designed to replace Capitalism and Free Enterprise with Technocracy.[55] It has exercised a relentless strategy using all the resources available to the UN. It is this latest iteration of this strategy that will be addressed in this chapter.

If Agenda 21 is viewed as a linear attack on humankind, then the major UN events of the last two years can be seen as a full-spectrum battle plan with three-dimensional characteristics. These events, which will now be discussed in detail, include,

1. UN Sustainable Development Summit held in New York on September 25-27, 2015 that produced the *2030 Agenda For Sustainable Development.*

2. UN Climate Change Conference held in Paris on November 30 through December 12, 2015, that produced the *Paris Agreement On Climate Change.*

3. Habitat III held in Quito, Ecuador on October 17-20, 2016 that produced the *New Urban Agenda.*

As you consider these three major UN events as a whole, you will note that a) the 2030 Agenda sets the overall goals and framework of Sustainable Development, b) the Paris Agreement provides the rationale for achieving the goals and c) the New Urban Agenda provides the action plan and specifics to implement it in every community on earth.

---

54 Ibid., p. 173.
55 The previous chapter recorded the UN's blunt intention to change the current economic model, transforming it into Sustainable Development, which is Technocracy.

The 2030 Agenda

Gro Harlem Brundtland, original editor/author of *Our Common Future* that gave rise to Agenda 21 in 1992, attended the UN Sustainable Development Summit in New York City. Brundtland's official title was "Special Envoy on Climate Change", indicating that she had a close working relationship with the head of Climate Change at the UN, Christiana Figueres. As the Summit ended on Sunday, September 27, 2015, Brundtland headed to Ohio State University to deliver a speech at Mershon Auditorium on the next day. The drumbeat was the same as she stated,

Finally, after nearly 30 years, countries all over the world have been able to overcome often very deep differences of opinion and priorities, and define common sustainable development goals, that apply to all countries, not just to the developing world... Indeed great strides have been fought, since the launch of the Millennium Development Goals in 2000. We have dramatically reduced the amount of people living in extreme poverty, more people have access to safe drinking water, fewer children are dying in infancy, and fewer mothers (are dying) when giving birth.[56]

But then she noted that "unprecedented levels of prosperity" had not been enough to narrow the gap between rich and poor, which was still "widening." Of course, it was still Climate Change that threatened the most vulnerable ecosystems and populations. What was the answer? More Development!

In fact, Brundtland's rosy economic picture was at odds with data published by the World Bank itself which is one of the most important drivers of globalization. From 1990 through 2015, the World Bank reports that the number of people living with under $10 per day had increased by 25 percent. Those living with under $5 per day had increased by 10 percent to include two-thirds of the earth's population.

The 2030 Agenda document that was produced at this Summit heralded 17 new and more comprehensive Sustainable

---

56 "Former Norwegian prime minister stresses sustainable development during speech", The Lantern, September 29, 2015.

Development Goals (SDGs). These replaced the so-called Millennium Development Goals (MDGs) that were created in 2000 and which were intended to expire in 2015. However, all UN literature was careful to state that the SDGs acknowledged and built upon both Agenda 21 and the MDGs. In other words, the SDGs represented a maturing and a natural expansion of the original Sustainable Development vision.

In light of Brundtland's vain attempt to outrun the real facts on global poverty, it is ironic that the very first SDG is a pledge to "End poverty in all its forms everywhere." One wonders what they will say in another 20 years when the poverty gap widens even more? Here are the 17 MDGs as drafted by the UN:

1. *End poverty in all its forms everywhere*

2. *End hunger, achieve food security and improved nutrition and promote sustainable agriculture*

3. *Ensure healthy lives and promote well-being for all at all ages*

4. *Ensure inclusive and equitable quality education and promote lifelong learning opportunities for all*

5. *Achieve gender equality and empower all women and girls*

6. *Ensure availability and sustainable management of water and sanitation for all*

7. *Ensure access to affordable, reliable, sustainable and modern energy for all*

8. *Promote sustained, inclusive and sustainable economic growth, full and productive employment and decent work for all*

9. *Build resilient infrastructure, promote inclusive and sustainable industrialization and foster innovation*

10. *Reduce inequality within and among countries*

11. *Make cities and human settlements inclusive, safe, resilient and sustainable*

12. *Ensure sustainable consumption and production patterns*

13. *Take urgent action to combat climate change and its impacts*

14. *Conserve and sustainably use the oceans, seas and marine resources for sustainable development*

15. *Protect, restore and promote sustainable use of terrestrial ecosystems, sustainably manage forests, combat deserti- fication, and halt and reverse land degradation and halt biodiversity loss*

16. *Promote peaceful and inclusive societies for sustainable development, provide access to justice for all and build ef- fective, accountable and inclusive institutions at all levels*

17. *Strengthen the means of implementation and revitalize the Global Partnership for Sustainable Development*

The first seven SDGs are purely Utopian speculations, designed to soften the psyche before pouring on the strong medicine. Only a fictional Utopia could end poverty and hunger, ensure health, water, provide lifelong education and full employment, etc. The word "development" finally appears in the eighth SDG, and the heart of the matter finally appears in SDG #12: *"Ensure sustain- able consumption and production patterns."* How will this be ac- complished?

The Preamble of the 2030 Agenda pledges that the UN is "deter- mined to protect the planet from degradation, including through sustainable consumption and production, *sustainably managing its natural resources*". Thus, the initial cost of Utopia is nothing less than turning over control of all natural resources to the UN. This thought is repeated in paragraph 33 of the Introduction,

We recognise that social and economic development depends on the sustainable management of our planet's natural re- sources. We are therefore determined to conserve and sus- tainably use oceans and seas, freshwater resources, as well as forests, mountains and drylands and to protect biodiversity, ecosystems and wildlife.[57]

Careful consideration of oceans, seas, freshwater, forests, mountains and drylands reveals that this represents 100 percent of the surface of earth. Subparagraph 12.2 of SDG 12 repeats the

---

57 "Transforming our world: the 2030 Agenda for Sustainable Development", Sustainable Development Knowledge Platform, UN.org.

thought yet again, "By 2030, achieve the sustainable management and efficient use of natural resources."

Someone is bound to rebut the thought that the UN will manage all global resources. Such a person is missing the strategy. Let's say you own property in a city or county that has adopted the UN's programs of Agenda 21, Smart Growth, Green Economy, etc., You will soon find yourself ensnared in a web of green regulations demanding that you manage your property according to their rules and guidelines. If you refuse, you will be fined, taxed, denied other rights and generally oppressed until you knuckle under and obey! While your name may be on the property title, your rights have been stripped and you have been forced to bow to UN-prescribed management practices. The point is, ownership and control of property are separate items.

International trade is also referenced as "an engine for inclusive economic growth and poverty reduction, and contributes to the promotion of Sustainable Development." Nations are encouraged to beat a path to the World Trade Organization (WTO) and to practice trade liberalization, or the removal or loosening of restrictions.

Lastly, and perhaps most importantly, science is put at center stage in Paragraph 70, and offered as the viable mechanism to achieve Sustainable Development. Since traditional solutions to overcome poverty, hunger, sickness, etc., have failed in the past, technology is viewed as the only possible savior. This smacks of Technocracy. More text is dedicated to this topic than any other portion of the 2030 Agenda document. *The UN Interagency Task Team on Science, Technology and Innovation* will work with 10 representatives from the civil society, private sector, and the scientific community to enable the SDGs world-wide. This massive endeavor will accumulate huge amounts of data, build giant databases and online sharing systems.

This was not lost on Technocrats outside the UN. One scientific group quickly concluded,

*The 2030 Agenda and its centrepiece, the Sustainable Development Goals (SDGs), call for a transformation in how societies interact with the planet and each other. This transformation will need new technologies, new knowledge and **new ways of structuring societies and economies.**[58]* [Emphasis added]

The UN issued a press release on the first day of the Summit before the ink was dry on the 2030 Agenda. If it were not for the discussion here, you would think that the world was saved and that Utopia had arrived:

A bold new global agenda to end poverty by 2030 and pursue a sustainable future was unanimously adopted today by the 193 Member States of the United Nations at the start of a three-day Summit on Sustainable Development.

The historic adoption of the new Sustainable Development Agenda, with 17 global goals at its core, was met with a thunderous standing ovation from delegations that included many of the more than 150 world leaders who will be addressing the Summit.

It was a scene that was, and will be, transmitted to millions of people around the world through television, social media, radio, cinema advertisements, and cell phone messages.

Secretary General Ban Ki-moon said, "It is an agenda for people, to end poverty in all its forms. It is an agenda for shared prosperity, peace and partnership (that) conveys the urgency of climate action (and) is rooted in gender equality and respect for the rights of all. Above all, it pledges to leave no one behind."[59]

Thus, the framework for global transformation by 2030 was chiseled on tablets like the Ten Commandments and were then held up for universal adoration.

But was the 2030 Agenda really hammered out by representatives from 195 nations as it was claimed? Hardly.

---

58 "How science should feed into 2030 Agenda", G.M.B. Akash, May 4, 2016, SciDev.Net website.
59 "Historic New Sustainable Development Agenda Unanimously Adopted by 193 UN Members", UN press release, Sept. 25, 2015.

The actual creation of the 2030 Agenda is easily traced[60] directly back to an earlier UN initiative called the *High-Level Panel of Eminent Persons on the Post-2015 Development Agenda* that met in July 2012 and concluded on May 30, 2013. There were only 27 elite members of this group, each handpicked from around the world and summarily appointed by the UN Director-General Ban Ki-moon.

The U.S. was represented by **John Podesta**, founder of the Center for American Progress and member of the elitist Trilateral Commission who subsequently went to work for President Obama as a Senior Policy Consultant on Climate Change. These 27 "eminent persons" delivered their concluding document to be formally ratified by yet another UN group, the *High-Level Political Forum on Sustainable Development* that met from June 26 through July 8, 2015.

After ratification, it was this very document that was presented for a global up-or-down vote on September 25 with no further changes allowed. This was hardly a democratic process. Essentially, it was just 27 people, including Trilateral **John Podesta**, who determined the framework for the world system.

In a side note, **John Podesta** has driven climate and environment policy in the US almost single-handedly for three decades. Under Bill Clinton, he implemented the "Roadless Rule" that shut down public roads within 59 million acres of U.S. Forest Service managed land. He also set policy for the establishment of 19 conservation areas and national monuments. While serving under Barack Obama he was behind the Executive Orders that created another 16 national monuments and he drove Obama's campaign to shut down the coal industry. In fact, Obama's entire environmental and climate change policy was attributed to Podesta. Fellow Trilateral Commission member **Bruce Babbitt**, who served as Secretary of the Interior under Bill Clinton, stated that "The hidden hand of John Podesta is involved in every envi-

---

60 See https://www.un.org/sg/en/management/beyond2015.shtml

ronmental advancement accomplished in the Clinton and Obama administrations."[61]

Paris Climate Agreement

Just six weeks after the close of the Sustainable Development Summit in New York, the UN Climate Change Conference convened in Paris, France on December 12, 2015. This gave birth to the *Paris Agreement On Climate Change*. The UN agency that sponsored this was the Framework Convention on Climate Change (UNFCCC), headed by Christiana Figueres. It is important to remember that Figueres is the same person who earlier called for the replacement of Capitalism and Free Enterprise with Sustainable Development.

The Paris Agreement was purposefully not called a treaty in order to avoid a ratification vote by the U.S. Senate, which most likely would have failed. The Senate and previous Administrations had resisted similar climate initiatives, such as the Kyoto Protocol adopted by the UN in Kyoto, Japan on December 11, 1997. According to the U.S. Constitution, all Treaties must be ratified by the Senate by two-thirds vote.

The strategy worked. On September 3, 2016, despite an outpouring of protests from Americans and elected representatives, President Obama took unilateral action by meeting in China with Premier Xi and a UN Delegation that included the Secretary-General, Ban Ki-moon. During that meeting, Obama signed the Paris Agreement, creating a legally-binding obligation for the American people.

The activation mechanism on the Paris Agreement was unique, requiring commitments from 55 nations that represent 55 percent of the carbon emissions of the entire world. Together, China and the U.S. represent approximately 40 percent of global emissions, so this signing ceremony pushed the Agreement to an earlier start than the original 2020 target. As a result, Obama and Xi

---

61 Shogren,"John Podesta: Legacy Maker", High Country News, May 25, 2015.

can rightfully claim that they were the global leaders who pushed the Paris Agreement into full force.

Undaunted by criticism at home, Obama bragged that "someday we may see this as the moment that we finally decided to save our planet."[62]

The 12-page Agreement contains 29 Articles that call for nations to

- Phase out greenhouse gas emissions to zero by 2050
- Implement policies to adapt development to climate change and plan for problems that are created by it
- Redirect financial funding away from dirty fossil fuels and towards clean forms of development
- Insure that all actions align with Paris and the Sustainable Development Goals of the 2030 Agenda.

In summary, the Paris Agreement solidified two key elements for the UN's planetary troika: first, fear of the consequences of inaction on climate change was made a permanent fixture throughout the world and second, it provided a succinct rationale for the need to implement the Sustainable Development Goals.

New Urban Agenda - Habitat III

The *United Nations Conference on Housing and Sustainable Urban Development* (Habitat III) was held in Quito, Ecuador from October 17-20, 2016, and produced its key document called *New Urban Agenda*. This was a monster meeting with over 30,000 people from 167 countries receiving UN accreditation to attend. There were 1,000 events, 8 plenary sessions, 6 high-level Roundtable sessions, 16 Stakeholder Roundtables, 22 Special Sessions, an Urban Journalism Academy and 59 UN events.[63] Plus, there were at least another 20,000 non-accredited attendees that participated in a host of unofficial gatherings around the city.

---

62 "President Obama: The United States Formally Enters the Paris Agreement", Sept. 3, 2016, See website www.obamawhitehouse.archives.gov.
63 See www.habitat3.org/the-new-urban-agenda website.

The resulting 2030 Agenda was 30 pages in length containing 175 paragraphs. Every conceivable aspect, feature and function of life is addressed in one way or another. As would be expected, science and technology are prominently featured, as is planning, trade, land use, energy and financing. Some areas deserve our special attention in this discussion.

Urban spatial planning. This term is often synonymous with urban planning but is especially focused on land use, transport and environmental planning. In particular, it focuses on influencing or manipulating the distribution of people within the community. The European Regional/Spatial Planning Charter states,

> *Regional/spatial planning gives geographical expression to the economic, social, cultural and ecological policies of society. It is at the same time a scientific discipline, an administrative technique and a policy developed as an interdisciplinary and comprehensive approach directed towards a balanced regional development and the physical organisation of space according to an overall strategy.*[64]

Whereas traditional planning was mostly an architectural practice, spatial planning has its roots in scientific discipline and is closely correlated with Technocracy.

Geospatial information systems. Stationary features of traditional geography are insufficient for urban spatial planning. People and vehicles move about, and so their 'geography' is changed from minute to minute. Geospatial information systems track the movement of people and things, and to the extent possible, the identity of the things being tracked. This is the main driver for the massive use of sensors in smart cities that track everything in real time, including people.

Urban and territorial planning. Within the discussion of urban spatial planning it is clearly stated that cities are not the only focus of the New Urban Agenda. It includes all adjacent territories, including rural areas. For instance, Paragraph 96 states, in part,

---

64 "Torremolinos Charter", European regional/spatial planning Charter, P. 13

*We will support the development of sustainable regional in-frastructure projects that stimulate sustainable economic productivity, promoting equitable growth of **regions across the urban-rural continuum.*** [emphasis added]

This points out the insufficiency of the title, New *Urban* Agenda because the Technocrat masters intend to control everything. Thus, if you live in a rural area, you will be arbitrarily assigned to a city region and will become subject to it rules, restrictions, land use policies, etc.

Science and Technology. The UN uses an acronym, STI, which stands for Science, Technology and Innovation, and it is actually the only hope, even if false, that Sustainable Development will ever work. Further, the hope is mostly in future technology that has not yet been developed or tested. This can be seen in the following Paragraphs:

157. We will support science, research and innovation, includ-ing a focus on social, technological, digital and nature-based innovation, robust science-policy interfaces in urban and ter-ritorial planning and policy formulation and institutional-ized mechanisms for sharing and exchanging information, knowledge and expertise, including the collection, analysis, standardization and dissemination of geographically based, community-collected, high-quality, timely and reliable data disaggregated by income, sex, age, race, ethnicity, migration status, disability, geographic location and other characteris-tics relevant in national, subnational and local contexts.

158. We will strengthen data and statistical capacities at the national, subnational and local levels to effectively monitor progress achieved in the implementation of sus-tainable urban development policies and strategies and to inform decision- making and appropriate reviews.

159. We will support the role and enhanced capacity of na-tional, subnational and local governments in data collec-tion, mapping, analysis and dissemination and in promoting evidence-based governance, building on a shared knowledge base using both globally comparable as well as locally gen-

erated data, including through censuses, household surveys, population registers, community-based monitoring process-es and other relevant sources, disaggregated by income, sex, age, race, ethnicity, migration status, disability, geographic location and other characteristics relevant in national, sub-national and local contexts.

No one left behind. This is also a key concept within the Sustainable Development Goals, that no one is left behind. A closely related word is "inclusive". Of course, if alleviating poverty is the goal, we would feel bad for anyone who might be left out, and likewise for the other Utopia-like goals: jobs with dignity, life-long educations, affordable housing, healthy life, etc. However, to a Technocrat, this phrase has a different meaning and purpose. The 1938 definition of Technocracy stated, "Technocracy is the science of social engineering, the scientific operation of the *entire* social mechanism to produce and distribute goods and services to the *entire* population..."[65] Note the use of "entire social mecha-nism" and "entire social population." It was a basic assumption of Technocracy that every single person *must be* included in their socially-engineered society; no exceptions or holdouts were al-lowed.

One academic journal hit the nail on the head when it wrote,

*Informal settlements house around one-quarter of the world's urban population. This means roughly 1 billion ur-ban dwellers live in settlements that have emerged **outside of the state's control.**[66] [emphasis added]*

There may be as many as 2 billion people, or 25 percent of earth's population, who currently live outside the system. Can you see the economic dilemma in the eyes of the global elite? Those outsiders don't contribute or add to the economy, but they do take up resources to survive. The answer? Paragraph 42 spins it this way: "Sustainable and inclusive urban prosperity and op-portunities for all."

65 "What is Technocracy", *The Technocrat Magazine*, 1930.
66 "When planning falls short: the challenges of informal settlements", *The Conversation*, December 5, 2016.

Conclusion

The purpose of this chapter is to reveal the latest monolithic strategy that has been launched by the United Nations in order to transform the world's economic system. This is the first stage of Christiana Figueres' boast on February 3, 2015 that they (the United Nations) were embarked on the task of "intentionally, within a defined period of time to change the economic development model that has been reigning for at least 150 years, since the industrial revolution." Thus, they revealed a) intention, b) a defined goal and c) a timeline. What more do we need to understand what is going on?

Virtually all of the UN, academic and NGO literature produced since the Habitat III conference has linked all three conferences together. It is a troika of coordinated strategy designed to accomplish specific goals within a particular time frame. The German Development Institute provided a perfect example:

> *Even if the Paris Agreement, 2030 Agenda and New Urban Agenda do not bring about a sustainable transformation in and of themselves, they provide major, internationally binding points of reference which can and must serve to catalyse transformative policies at all levels of action. In order to integrate climate, sustainability and urbanisation agendas in a targeted way to this end, it is pivotal for each of the multilateral pledges to develop an impact at national and local levels.*[67]

Indeed, these three conferences have reenergized, refocused and re-strategized the entire planet into a single-minded agenda: Technocracy, aka Sustainable Development.

---

67 "Paris Climate Agreement, 2030 Agenda and New Urban Agenda: the future of transformative policies", German Development Institute Annual Report 2015-2016, P. 17.

CHAPTER 4

THE RISE OF THE GLOBAL CITY

*The world city as an analytical concept was developed
in the 1970s and caught on in the 1980s as a new frame
within which to grasp globalization.*[90]

When the Trilateral Commission was established in 1973, interdependence between nation-states was never a fait accompli, but it was nonetheless heavily promoted by the Commission and its members as being true. As the Commission subsequently began to gain political influence in the three main trading areas of the world (Japan, North America and Europe), several things were put into action.

First, protectionist mechanisms and trade barriers such as tariffs and import taxes began to fall under the guise of 'Free Trade'. Second, trade agreements were created that forced signers to adhere to common trading rules. This gave rise, for instance, to the World Trade Organization (WTO) in 1995. Third, a process of deregulation of industries was instituted that effectively nullified the power of nation-states to regulate commerce.

---

90 Clark , Greg (2016-11-29). Global Cities: A Short History (The Short Histories) (p. 95). Brookings Institution Press.

In the United States, it was President **James Earl Carter** who finally kick-started deregulation of the Transportation industry. Major intellectual studies were produced by the University of Chicago (tightly associated with Rockefeller interests), the Brookings Institution (also associated with Rockefeller interests) and the American Enterprise Institute. Before his term completed, Carter had sponsored and signed the *Airline Deregulation Act* in October 1978, the *Staggers Rail Act* in October 1980 and the *Motor Carrier Act* in July 1980.

But, it didn't stop with Carter. Ronald Reagan (with Vice-President **George H.W. Bush**, a Trilateral member) went on to support and sign the *Bus Regulatory Reform Act of 1982*, the Ocean Shipping Act of 1984 and the *Surface Freight Forwarder Deregulation Act of 1986*.

Last, Trilateral Commission member and President **William Jefferson Clinton** promoted and signed the *Ocean Shipping Reform Act of 1998*.

What was one of the key elements to globalized 'Free Trade'? *Transportation!* Why was this industry deregulated? To take it out of the hands of the government and turn it over to the industry itself. Thus, they could set their own regulations, processes and rates as it suited their interests. Interdependence between nations was well on its way to becoming a reality.

The next three major industries to be deregulated included Energy, Communications and Finance. Taken together with Transportation, this completes the view of what globalists call *'infrastructure'*. Government was stripped of its regulatory authority, which was ceded lock, stock and barrel to the cause of globalization, run by the same global elite who were dedicated to creating the Trilateral Commission's *New International Economic Order*.

Well, of course they wanted control over the infrastructure! They couldn't move forward without it. And because there were three regions represented in the Trilateral Commission membership, it shouldn't be a surprise to learn that similar legislation and deregulation took place in Japan and Europe as well where governments had been similarly infiltrated by the local Commission members. Thus, this provided for a common infrastructure between the trading partners, insuring quick and reliable transportation of goods and services without meddling interference from national governments. In modern parlance, this is collectively called the 'supply chain'.

Infrastructure is going to be a major theme in this book because it is one of the most hotly debated and sought after topics in the world of globalization. Today, however, the bulk of discussion about infrastructure has pivoted away from the nation-state toward global cities. It is cities that must have fluid infrastructure internally and also externally in order to connect them into networks of cities. It is cities that must be managed, squeezing out inefficiencies and excesses in order to milk the maximum amount of profit from each square mile.

Cities of the past were operated by elected representatives of the people who were responsive to citizen needs and aspirations. Cities of the future will increasingly be run by corporations, investors and social engineers who have different ends in mind. How is this so? First, external parties plant expectations that a certain level of infrastructure is needed in order to stay competitive and grow. Second, as the cities face their own reality of insufficient capital to build out such a grandiose infrastructure, Public-Private Partnerships are offered as a means of finance and development expertise. Funds are then provided by 'private' parties to complete infrastructure projects with a long list of extra conditionalities that essentially diminish sovereignty for the people and increase control of the non-elected parties. In other words, cities are being taken over by those entities who want to **use the resources of the cities to serve their own ends.**

One key side-effect of globalization has been to drive rural people into cities. Major factories or high-tech startups are rarely found in rural areas. Indeed, commerce is often tightly correlated to population centers. On one hand, cities provide labor pools to tap into in order to scale smaller enterprises into larger ones. On the other hand, people seeking their fortune gravitate to cities to find better jobs and opportunities. In addition, Gen-Xers through Millennials are often attracted to urban living because of lifestyle, cultural opportunities and relationships.

When we lay modern globalization at the feet of members of groups like the Trilateral Commission, we don't have to speculate as to whether or not this was an intended policy: it *was*!

In 1992, the Agenda 21 document stated, for instance,

By the turn of the century, the majority of the world's popula-
tion will be living in cities. While urban settlements, particu-
larly in developing countries, are showing many of the symp-
toms of the global environment and development crisis, they
nevertheless generate 60 per cent of gross national product
and, if properly managed, can develop the capacity to sustain
their productivity, improve the living conditions of their resi-
dents and manage natural resources in a sustainable way.[91]

Because 60 percent of economic activity was seen as being generated in cities, the majority of future economic growth would likewise come from cities. With rural areas producing dispropor-tionately to their population, there was only one way to increase overall productivity, namely, to increase the density of existing cities and move more people into them. The above condition "if properly managed" provides insight into the modern movement toward Global Cities (of size) which are also Smart Cities (of de-sign).

Twenty years later in 2002, the global consulting firm McKinsey & Company narrowed the focus by stating that "over the next 13 years, 600 cities will account for nearly 65 percent of global GDP growth."[92] More recently it noted that "by 2025 megacities of 10 million or more people will house more than half the world's population and contribute more than half of global GDP."[93]

In 2016 the World Economic Forum provides the latest insight:

---

91 United Nations, Agenda 21, Improving Human Settlement Management, Basis for Action, Section B.7.13.

92 McKinsey&Co., Global cities of the future: An interactive map, June, 2012. (See http://www. mckinsey.com/global-themes/urbanization/global-cities-of-the-future-an-interactive-map)

93 McKinsey&Co., *Sustainable Cities*, Website http://www.mckinsey.com/

Our cities cover just 2% of the Earth's surface, but are currently home to more than 50% of the world's population, generate more than 80% of the world's GDP, use 75% of the world's natural resources, consume 75% of global energy supply and produce approximately 75% of global CO2 emissions.[94]

Thus, the GDP concentration of cities rose from 60% to 65% to 80% in the span of 28 years. Is this really the case or just wishful thinking? Probably a little of both, but it is clearly the perception of the global elite.

Indeed, cities are increasingly seen as the *only* fertile harvest ground of profit for global corporations which is precisely why the entire universe of development wonks are focused on developing cities. This includes the myriads of NGOs, universities, think-tanks, the United Nations, global corporations and consultant groups like McKinsey. In the latter's case, one can see the green gleam in their eyes when they write,

To support our work with clients, we carry out independent research and draw on an extensive body of in-house knowledge. The McKinsey Global Institute has conducted studies of urbanization in China, India, and Latin America, and its work on cities globally has culminated in City Scope, the largest database of its kind, covering more than 2,000 metropolitan areas. We also play an active part in the debate on the future of cities through collaborations with non-profits, foundations, and think tanks. Our partnership with Columbia University and Tsinghua University in the Urban China Initiative led to the development of the urban sustainability index, a new tool for evaluating how cities in developing countries are balancing growth and sustainability.[95]

More specifically, McKinsey lists its offerings to cities and related parties:

---

94 World Economic Forum, "As the world descends on Ecuador, what is Habitat III?", Alice Charles, October 17, 2016.
95 Ibid.

We work with mayors, urban planners, foundations, nonprofits, utilities, and businesses to help create sustainable cities. Our role includes:

- *supporting mayors and city authorities in establishing a fact base, defining sustainable economic development, and delivering solutions tailored to local needs*

- *working with water, power, and waste utilities to improve services, minimize waste, and reduce a city's environmental footprint*

- *assisting private sector clients such as real-estate developers, infrastructure providers, and logistics companies in engaging with cities and creating solutions that support sustainability goals*

- *helping shape strategies to capture growth opportunities by developing district development plans, revitalizing older cities, and building greenfield cities that minimize their carbon footprint while attracting new jobs and industries*[96]

*This **emerging science of global cities** is being pursued in different places through an increasingly connected global community of scholars and analysts that includes at least the Chinese Academy of Sciences in Beijing, the Mori Memorial Foundation in Tokyo, the Brookings Institution and the World Bank in Washington, D.C., the Organization for Economic Cooperation and Development in Paris, UN-Habitat in Nairobi, the wider United Nations and the Ford Foundation in New York, the LSE Cities Group in London, the McKinsey Global Institute in New York, the World Economic Forum in Geneva, United Cities and Local Governments in Barcelona, and the African Centre for Cities in Cape Town. In addition to this work are more than 200 indexes, benchmark reports, and global reviews of cities that are produced by a wide range of organizations, including the Globalization and World Cities Group, the Financial Times, the Economist, Jones Lang LaSalle, Mercer, Mastercard, PricewaterhouseCoopers,*

---

96 Ibid.

the Chicago Council on Global Affairs, and many more.[97] *[emphasis added]*

The 'emerging science of global cities' belongs solely to the realm of Technocrats and their practitioners. It harkens back to the 1937 definition of Technocracy,

Technocracy is the science of social engineering, the scientific operation of the entire social mechanism to produce and distribute goods and services to the entire population of this continent. For the first time in human history it will be done as a scientific, technical, engineering problem.[98]

UN Habitat-III

The United Nations first fixed its eyes squarely on urban development with the establishment of the *United Nations Habitat and Human Settlements Foundation* (UNHHSF) on January 1, 1975, just eight months after passing Resolution 3201: *Declaration on the Establishment of a New International Economic Order.* At the time, UNHHSF was placed under the UN Environmental Programme (UNEP), but after the first international conference (Habitat I) was held in Vancouver, Canada in 1976, it took on a life of its own as the *Commission on Human Settlements and the Centre for Human Settlements.*

Habitat II was held twenty years later in 1996 in Istanbul, Turkey and incorporated the newly minted Sustainable Development and Agenda 21 doctrines that originated from the Rio Declaration on Environment and Development held in 1992.

Finally, on January 1, 2002, the UN passed General Assembly Resolution A/56/206 that officially birthed UN-Habitat, the *United Nations Human Settlements Programme*, as a full fledged program within the UN system.

The scope and influence of UN-Habitat is immense within the UN framework and in terms of global influence. According the the current UN-Habitat web site,

---

97 Op cit. , p. 6.
98 *The Technocrat Magazine*, Technocracy, Inc., Vol. 3, No. 4, September 1937.

"UN-Habitat, the United Nations Human Settlements Programme, is mandated by the UN General Assembly to promote socially and environmentally sustainable towns and cities. It is the focal point for all urbanization and human settlement matters within the UN system."[99]

In October 2016, twenty years after Habitat II, the third iteration of Habitat (predictably called Habitat-III) was held in Quito, Ecuador and the nation-members of the world signed onto its key document called the *New Urban Agenda*.

The calls to action contained in the New Urban Agenda are clear and comprehensive:

We adopt this New Urban Agenda as a collective vision and political commitment to promote and realize sustainable urban development, and as a historic opportunity to leverage the key role of cities and human settlements as drivers of sustainable development in an increasingly urbanized world.

Furthermore, it reiterated that its scope is

universal, participatory and people-centred, protects the planet and has a long-term vision, setting out priorities and actions at the global, regional, national, subnational and local levels that Governments and other relevant stakeholders in every country can adopt based on their needs.

In essence, this historic compact gives the UN the right to impose its Sustainable Development action plan in every local community on the planet, and this is exactly what it plans to do.

However, it is misguided to think that the New Urban Agenda is about cities only while ignoring the rural world. Paragraph 49 makes this painfully clear:

We commit ourselves to supporting territorial systems that integrate urban and rural functions into the national and subnational spatial frameworks and the systems of cities and human settlements, thus promoting sustainable management and use of natural resources and land, ensuring reliable supply and value chains that connect urban and rural supply and demand to foster equitable regional development across

---

99 Website, https://unhabitat.org/.

the urban-rural continuum and fill social, economic and territorial gaps.

Thus, the city is seen at the center of all surrounding rural acreage, which is blithely swept into the city's web of control. Rural areas will simply be assigned to their proximate city and then fall under all the same rules and regulations that control the city. Not content with just rural control, the New Urban Agenda expands further to "sustainable management of resources, including land, water (oceans, seas and freshwater), energy, materials, forests and food."

Globalist rhetoric is seen peeking through with statements like "facilitating effective trade links across the urban-rural continuum and ensuring that small-scale farmers and fishers are linked to local, subnational, national, regional and global value chains and markets." [emphasis added]

In total, there are 175 numbered statements in the New Urban Agenda. Some are meaningless platitudes but others contain the hard-core intent. When taken as a whole without any preconceived ideas, the UN is promoting globalization from start to finish, where cities become tightly-run work centers or labor camps, supply chains deliver products to and from other cities with maximum precision and all rural areas are enlisted to keep the urban bound workers nourished and pacified.

For those who have ever worried that the United Nations promotes some sort of global political system, that could not be further from the truth. Sustainable Development is purely economic, not political, and it is designed to serve the economic and monetary interests of the global corporate community. It does not return political power to the citizenry but rather usurps it by vesting control to corporate Technocrats through Public-Private Partnerships.

1976	UN Habitat I, Vancouver, Canada. The first UN conference on Human Settlements
1992	Agenda 21: Rio Declaration on Environment and Development
1996	UN Habitat II, Istanbul, Turkey

2000	Millennium Development Goals (MDGs)
2001	Habitat +5 Review. Appraising progress of five years after Habitat II
2002	World Urban Forum (WUF). The first session of WUF
2012	Rio+20: UN Conference on Sustainable Development. Stated that the battle for sustainable development will be won or lost in the cities.
2015	Sustainable Development Goals (SDGs). Replaced MDGs from 2000 and created a standalone goal (11) on cities
2016	Habitat III: The third UN conference on Human Settlements.

Table 1: Timeline of Key UN Events

New Urban Agenda

Formalized in October 2016, the New Urban agenda has been billed as being "responsible for establishing the policy frameworks that will guide the governance of the world's cities for the coming 20 years."[100]

This may seem a bit egotistical and grandiose, but this is the stated goal of the UN and all of its stakeholder organizations. It seeks to impose a common framework that all cities, large or small, will follow. It includes all the supporting principles of the 1992 Agenda 21, the 2030 Agenda created in 2017 and its 17 Sustainable Development Goals. Indeed, the New Urban Agenda is the capstone of all preceding efforts to control humanity, and is much more comprehensive than any previous attempts.

The New Urban Agenda is also a massive power grab. The official document uses the word 'regional' 45 times. The word 'local' appears 138 times and subnational 64 times. The phrase 'local and regional government" is mentioned 8 times. On the other hand, the word 'national' is mentioned only 73 times and usually within the context of the smaller entities. This is clearly designed to encourage cities to take control over their own destinies and to shun state or national control.

Thus, a city can now unilaterally declare itself to be a 'sanctuary city' even it is defies immigration law or the Constitution. Over 240 cities declared support for the Paris Climate Agreement even

---

100 RioOnWatch, The Future of Urban Policy: The UN's New Urban Agenda, (http://www.rioonwatch.org/?p=31275).

though it defied national policy of having withdrawn from the accord. Many larger cities and states have negotiated their own trade agreements with foreign governments, even though Federal law prohibits it. Most U.S. cities have implemented General Plans that contain policies derived directly from the United Nations' Agenda 21, 2030 Agenda, Sustainable Development, New Urban Agenda, etc.

Cities today are seeking their own identity and control over their own destiny regardless of national or state authority to the contrary. The larger the city, the stronger the rebellion. In recent years, the concept of a city-state (a city that with its surrounding territory forms an independent state) only applied to Singapore, Monaco and Vatican City. Today, New York, Los Angeles, San Francisco and others are speaking about themselves in terms of the city-state. This doesn't mean that they have arrived, but it certainly highlights the struggle to get free from all other constraints and enter into the elite of other global cities of equal magnitude.

How have so many American cities been seduced into these un-American, anti-Free Enterprise policies? We need to look no further than to a non-governmental organization (NGO) called ICLEI, which originally was an acronym standing for International Council for Local Environmental Initiatives. It now defines itself as "Local Governments for Sustainability."

ICLEI has huge influence over 12 mega-cities, 100 super-cities, 450 large cities and 650 smaller cities in 80 countries.[101] ICLEI's services to cities are comprehensive:

> *ICLEI works to help local governments achieve a more sustainable future for their communities, through reductions in greenhouse gas emissions, water or waste management, sustainable procurement, securing biodiversity and many other tangible improvements in local sustainability. To help local governments to meet their **self-defined goals**, we provide software tools, trainings, technical assistance, guidebooks, as*

---

well as vibrant peer networks where local government staff
can share challenges and best practices.[102] [emphasis added]

However, ICLEI is completely disingenuous about a local government's 'self-defined goals' because the only goals available to choose from are the 17 Sustainable Development Goals published by the UN. If *those* are your goals, then ICLEI will happily smother you with rhetoric, tools, consultants and conferences all designed to transform your city into a model of Sustainable Development. If those are not your goals, ICLEI will drop you like a hot potato.

ICLEI is unabashed in its support of local governments only. It completely bypasses all national governments and speaks directly to local officials. It is not insignificant that ICLEI hides behind the phrase 'voluntary participation' so that nobody can accuse it of forcing policies down anyone's throat. In a sense, this is true because ICLEI has no authority to do anything for anybody: they simply whisper in a city manager's ear how great it would be if his or her city were sustainable.

This writer has had experience with one city's general plan where a sustainability consultant from out of town presented the city manager with a dilemma. The consultant asserted that it was just a matter of time before they were massively sued by some environmental organization over environmental abuses, and the only way they could prepare to defend against such lawsuits would be to have a General Plan in place that focuses on Sustainable Development. Of course, only that consultant's company had the skills to create such a General Plan that would offer the proper protection. The veiled threat of certain harm in order to sell a particular General Plan is akin to extortion, but it has worked time after time in cities and towns across America, to the extent that one can hardly find a plan that isn't riddled with Agenda 21 and Sustainable Development policies... all 'voluntary', of course!

All of the New Urban Agenda network is designed to support the upward progression of cities toward becoming global cities. There may be many stages and necessary transformations in or-

---

102 Ibid.

der to get there, but the road map is provided. According to Dr. Parag Khanna, who ranks cities based on goods, services, capital, people and data, there are currently only eight world-class global cities: San Francisco, Los Angeles, New York, London, Dubai, Shanghai, Hong Kong and Singapore. Other experts would include Seoul, Toronto, Zurich, Beijing and Helsinki. Is your city a wannabe global player? Then these are the cities that you must connect with.

One thing is certain, however: all global cities are, by definition, controlled by Sustainable Development, Agenda 21, 2030 Agenda and the New Urban Agenda. In the transition, cities are intended to replace the nation-state as the primary unit of global organizational structure. World Economic Forum noted that ICLEI is not alone in the drive to restructure the world:

> *There are already over 200 inter-city networks around the world that are agitating for a new urban agenda. One of the most prominent, United Cities and Local Government seeks to promote connectivity between cities and agitate on behalf of them. A new coalition called the Global Parliament of Mayors is also urging cities everywhere to take advantage of the devolution revolution. After all cities no longer need to wait and ask for permission to exert their urban sovereignty.[103]*

The New Urban Agenda is a framework for the social organization people in cities regardless of population. It specified three guiding principles:

1. Leave no one behind, ensure urban equality and eradicate poverty

2. Achieve sustainable and inclusive urban prosperity and opportunities for all

3. Foster ecological and resilient cities and human settlements.

The World Economic Forum describes the three key components that would provide the direction for this transformation:

---

103 *Cities, not nation states, will determine our future survival*, World Economic Forum, June 2, 2017.

- ***Urban Rules and Regulations***: *The outcomes in terms of quality of urban settlement depend on the set of rules and regulations that are framed and made effective. Strengthening urban legislation, providing predictability and directive to the urban development plans to enable social and economic progression.*

- ***Urban Planning and Design***: *Strengthen urban and territorial planning to best utilize the spatial dimension of the urban form and deliver the urban advantage.*

- ***Municipal Finance***: *Establishing effective financing frameworks, enabling strengthened municipal finance and local fiscal systems in order to create, sustain and share the value generated by sustainable urban development.*[104]

As simple as these sound, they cover 100 percent of the requirements for urban transformation: **Regulations, Design and Finance.** All three of these can be seen in Paragraph 5 of the NUA: *"By readdressing the way cities and human settlements are planned, designed, financed, developed, governed and managed, the New Urban Agenda will help to...".* This is not just a few helpful tips or useful resources, but rather a total rewrite of city life from the ground up. To make it somehow palatable to the reader, the platitudes are then poured on:

> *"...will help to **end poverty and hunger** in all its forms and dimensions; **reduce inequalities**; promote sustained, inclusive and **sustainable economic growth**; achieve **gender equality** and the empowerment of all women and girls in order to fully harness their vital contribution to sustainable development; improve **human health** and wellbeing; foster **resilience**; and **protect the environment**. [emphasis added]*

In other words, if you want to end poverty, have good health and protect the environment, then you should simply turn your city over to them to be "planned, designed, financed, developed, governed and managed" *by* them for your benefit. Who would fall

---

104 World Economic Forum, "As the world descents on Equador, what is Habitat III?", Alice Charles, October 17, 2016.

for such a thinly disguised con game? Apparently the 167 nations who signed the document.

This proposition is repeated in Paragraph 15 by promising to *"Readdress the way we **plan, finance, develop, govern and manage cities and human settlements**, recognizing sustainable urban and territorial development as essential to the achievement of sustainable development and prosperity for all."* [emphasis added]

Miscellany

Dr. William Levingston was actually an itinerant salesman with a phony name who created a concoction of oil and laxative and branded it as a cure for cancer. Since cancer was a dreaded and usually fatal disease, people would buy and try literally anything for a cure. He would explain that if his miracle cure was strong enough to beat cancer, then it would most certainly take care of a whole lot of other diseases as well! When William came to a new town, he would mesmerize and trick people into buying his "miracle cure." As soon as anyone questioned the his phony operation, he would ride out much faster than he had originally arrived. William was indeed a fraud and a con artist, but he somehow always managed to escape arrest or lynching. He died in 1906 at the ripe old age of 95. Earlier in life, he reportedly bragged "I cheat my boys every chance I get. I want to make 'em sharp."

However, Levingston's name was indeed a fraud. His real name was William Avery Rockefeller, Sr. and one of those 'sharp' sons was John D. Rockefeller, who was soon to become the richest man in America and grandfather of David A. Rockefeller, founder of the Trilateral Commission in 1973.

The entire fraud being perpetrated by the United Nations, with its deep roots into the Rockefeller family and with its modern genesis in the Trilateral Commission and Technocracy, smacks of the Rockefeller snake-oil legacy dating all the way up the family tree into the 1800s.

The structure of today's con is the same even if the scale of it is far greater: Utopia is yours if you simply give up control over all your production and consumption, ie, the entire economy of the world! Unfortunately, people are just as gullible today as they were back then.

CHAPTER 5

THE SMART CITY STEAMROLLER

In the end, the smart city will destroy democracy. Like Google, they'll have enough data not to have to ask you what you want.[113] *- Leo Hollis*

When I was around twelve years old, I apparently said something in resistance against my mother's authority and she replied, "Don't get smart with me, buster." A couple of years later, a teacher commented that I was very smart and congratulated me on getting a good grade. Here we see two very different semantic usages of the same word even though both are applied to a person and not a thing.

When it comes to the term "Smart City", what does smart mean? A city is a thing but is full of people; does it mean that all the people who live there are smart? Not likely. The most common thinking is that it is used as a contrast against the word "dumb", where a smart city does things in an intelligent way but non-smart cities are reckoned to be dumb, backward or ignorant. This is actually a clever marketing nudge to get people to think favorably about the term without having the slightest idea of what it really means. After all, who wants to live in a "dumb city"? Of course, we all want our city to be smart!

To the global corporate giants who are relentlessly promoting and designing today's smart cities, S.M.A.R.T. is a commonly used acronym in project management jargon that stands for Specific, Measurable, Attainable, Relevant and Timely. Once you see this, you cannot unsee it: the global behemoths view the city as nothing more than a technology project where the herd of inhabitants must be micromanaged to achieve *Attainable* and *Relevant* goals in a *Timely* manner. As expected, monitoring technology and ubiquitous data collection are always woven into the city's fabric in order to provide *Measurable* results.

It is helpful at this point to remember *The Technocrat*'s 1938 definition of Technocracy:

> *Technocracy is the science of social engineering, the scientific operation of the entire social mechanism to produce and distribute goods and services to the entire population...*[114]

In short, smart city dogma is an application of the "science of social engineering." The target is the entire social unit, in this case, the city. The object is to provide goods and services to all of its inhabitants.

Who are these global corporations that champion smart cities? Here are a few notable leaders: IBM, Cisco, Siemens, Huawei, Microsoft, Nvidia, Hitachi and Oracle. For instance, Siemens' website states,

> *Urbanization, climate change, and globalization are posing multiple challenges to cities and city stakeholders. Ensuring mobility, improving energy efficiency, and increasing the economic value of buildings are among the main priorities when it comes to creating and managing urban infrastructure. Through digitalization, we enable cities to optimize the performance of buildings, transport and energy systems, while ensuring the safety and security of people and assets.*[115]

A 2013 press release from IBM notes that,

> *IBM is helping cities around the world use the vast amount of information already available to deliver more efficient citi-*

---
114 *The Technocrat magazine*, 1938
115https://www.siemens.com/global/en/home/company/ fairs-events/scewc.html

zen services. IBM's experience with cities continuously fuels more effective solutions and best practices to help city leaders transform their communities.[116]

A blog article on Nvidia's website declares,

Alibaba and Huawei join more than 50 of the world's leading companies already using NVIDIA Metropolis[117]. Together, we're taking advantage of the more than 1 billion video cameras that will be in our cities by the year 2020 to solve a dizzying array of problems.[118]

You should get the idea that there is a feeding frenzy among smart city players to capture as much as possible of the $600 billion per year market. This is a market growing at an estimated twenty-four percent per year that will reach $2 trillion by 2023.[119] The prestigious Mordor Intelligence further describes the scenario:

*Smart Cities and Internet of Things (IoT) are on their way to **transform modern life**. Smart Cities make effective use of IoT. IoT instills the required intelligence into **basic building blocks of the city**, and helps make it smart. In 2017, Smart Cities occupied major share in IoT. Smart Cities is expected to utilize IoT to monitor energy usage, traffic flows, and water levels etc. The effective use of IoT in Smart Cities is totally reliant on the infrastructure development, and smart supply chain.*[120] [emphasis added]

The ambitions of Smart City Technocrats must not be trivialized. They intend to *"transform modern life"* by integrating data collected from all devices connected to the so-called Internet of Things, into AI programs that act as control centers for various city functions.

What is the Internet of Things (IoT)? It is the network of physical devices such as appliances, smartphones, vehicles, sensors,

116 IBM Brings All The Pieces of the Smart City Puzzle Together, IBM, 13 Aug. 2013.
117 Metropolis is an advanced Artificial Intelligence system developed by NVIDIA to perform Smart City functions.
118 Alibaba, Huawei Adopt NVIDIA's Metropolis AI Smart Cities Platform, Saurabh Jain, 25 Sept. 2017.
119 "Global Smart Cities Market", *Mordor Intelligence*, March 2018.
120 Ibid.

actuators, RFID embedded chips, surveillance cameras, license plate readers, listening devices, etc. These devices receive and transmit data via WiFi or cellular connection.

In one article, *"NVIDIA's plan to turn data from 500 million cameras into AI gold"*, it is noted that there will be one billion surveillance cameras installed globally by 2020.[121] That's one camera for every seven or eight humans on earth! The amount of data generated from these cameras is incomprehensible, but using advanced AI tuned especially for images and running on its computer chips, NVIDIA will give its city-clients tools to track everyone, everywhere and in real time.

The Smart Grid initiative started in 2009 by President Barack Obama kick started the IoT for energy. By now, most Americans have seen WiFi-enabled Smart Meters installed on their homes and businesses. These meters are a gateway to collect data from energy-consuming appliances and also to transmit commands to regulate them. Theoretically, every refrigerator washer, dryer, thermostat, motor, computer or TV can be monitored continuously and simultaneously by your local utility and anyone else they choose to send your data to.

As autonomous vehicles gain market influence, they will be connected to a central control point but also to each other as they move about on city streets. Immense amounts of data will be collected and analyzed in real time.

Smartphones are already connecting hundreds of millions of people with not only other people but also with their inanimate devices like health and fitness tracking and smart home devices, their cars, sound systems, etc.

Collectively, all of these devices are considered the IoT, which Mordor claims "instills the required intelligence into **basic building blocks of the city**, and helps make it smart." Building blocks, large or small, are the elements that construct a city from the top down and bottom up, using advanced technology as the mortar.

This is exactly how these giant tech companies approach the problem of city design and urban planning.

In fact, entire cities are being created from scratch to showcase Smart City technology. The city of Songdo was founded in 2003 as a public-private partnership within a Free Economic Zone (FEZ) in South Korea. It sits on 1,400 acres, has room for 250,000 citizens, all of whom will be under constant surveillance by 500 cameras. It is also home to the United Nations' Global Institute for Green Growth. Songdo is called the "City of the Future", "The World's Smartest City" and "Korea's High-Tech Utopia." After 15 years of constant development however, Songdo only has a population of 70,000 to enjoy its ubiquitous Internet and built-in video wall communication centers.

Critics have less than glowing assessments for Songdo. The International New Town Institute based in The Netherlands states,

> *These cities (Songdo) look like the CIAM-inspired modernist cities from the 1960s—as if we've learned nothing over the last half-century of urban planning innovation. This typology was, indeed, once seen as a panacea for cities everywhere, but is now considered a failed model that has cost some communities a heavy price. Many sociologists and historians now blame this model for rising crime rates, social exclusion, limited access to public amenities and heightened class divisions.*

CIAM refers to the Congrès Internationaux d'Architecture Moderne (International Congresses of Modern Architecture) that operated between 1928 and 1959, and where famous architects of the day posed as urban planners. CIAM projects failed miserably and its entire urban design philosophy was largely discredited. Leading intellectuals of the day heavily promoted CIAM as a new approach to planning human settlements: Barbara Ward, Margaret Mead, Buckminster Fuller and Arnold Toynbee.

The New Town Institute finally concluded that "the planned towns and cities we now see coming up across Asia and Africa are almost exclusively for the wealthy."[122]

---

122 International New Town Institute, *When Smart Cities are Stupid*, Rachael Keeton, 2012.

In 2017, Bill Gates committed $80 million to create a smart city called Belmont in the Arizona desert west of Phoenix. Forty square miles of sand and desert flora will be transformed into a high-tech metropolis of 160,000 inhabitants. According to a press release, Belmont will be

A forward-thinking community with a communication and infrastructure spine that embraces cutting-edge technology, designed around high-speed digital networks, data centers, new manufacturing technologies and distribution models, autonomous vehicles and autonomous logistics hubs.[123]

The official term coined by Technocrats to refer to Smart Cities is *urbanates,* and this is where history meets the future. The few original Technocrats remaining from the last century who were associated with Technocracy, Inc., have argued with this writer that their pure form of Technocracy has nothing to do with the modern implementation of Technocracy via globalization, Agenda 21, 2030 Agenda or Sustainable Development. Their protest is nonsense. While there is little doubt that these early Technocrats had any modern direct ties to tech giants like IBM or NVIDIA, their own literature gives a succinct definition of urbanates:

Urbanates are Technocracy's solution to most of the problems found in the major cities of today. Briefly, urbanates would have the following properties:

- *Small size (perhaps 20,000-100,000 people)*
- *Planned, top-down design*
- *Pre-installed, integrated transportation, utilities, and communications*
- *Safe, pollution free environment*

No more traffic jams, smog, long travel times, and lack of parking spaces, which are just some of the benefits of urbanates. Their overall design philosophy is scientific, and their final design will provide the citizens living in them with these advantages in accord with the goals of Technocratic living. By being planned from the start, Urbanates do not con-

123 CBS Moneywatch, Bill Gates spends $80 million to create a "smart city" in Arizona, Nov. 13, 2017.

stantly expand in a random fashion that necessitates the use of inefficient forms of transportation, such as the automobile. Urbanates would instead employ a functional and convenient form of mass-transit that may resemble a cross between a subway system and elevators. Combined with its small size making most destinations within walking distance, transportation in an Urbanate would be quick and worry free. They would also contain all of the distribution, health care, education, and recreation centers that would be needed and desired by the population of these cities of the future.[124]

An insightful book, *Against The Smart City* by Adam Greenfield, analyzes the modern Smart City and concludes,

The notion of the smart city in its full contemporary form appears to have originated within these businesses, rather than with any party, group or individual, recognized for their contributions to the theory or practice of urban planning. That is, the enterprises enumerated here are to a surprisingly great degree responsible for producing both the technical systems on which the smart city is founded and the rhetoric that binds them together as a conceptual whole.[125]

A respected urban planning expert, Greenfield further explains that the ideas at the core of today's Smart City practice originated during the eighty years between 1880 and 1960 when the so-called "high-modernism" in urban planning was incubated, hatched and ultimately failed:

The descriptions of the serene and masterful guidance of the city-as-machine-for-living we hear about from Siemens or Cisco or IBM are strikingly reminiscent of LeCorbusier (CIAM). What we see in the smart-city material across the board is a straight and occasionally even naive rendition of tropes that were taken to pieces fifty years ago.[126]

The point of this discussion is to clearly show that the modern Smart City theory and practice is *not* revolutionary thinking as is claimed by proponents, but rather is hijacked from failed theory

---

124 Urbanates, Technocracy.ca website
125 Adam Greenfield, Against the Smart City, Do Projects, 2013, p.161 (Kindle).
126 Ibid., p. 1263 (Kindle).

and practice from the last century. Today's Smart Cities will not and indeed, cannot, deliver on their promise of urban Utopia.

Nevertheless, given the power and intent within the big-tech companies, we marvel at how successful their propaganda has been to sell Smart Cities as the *cities of the future*, boldly going where no society has gone before. If history is a guide, this will not end well for people living in these cities.

Who is paying for all this new or retrofitted construction of Smart Cities? Certainly not the cities themselves! In the United States, cities are already swamped with debt, unfunded liabilities, and deferred maintenance projects on roads, bridges, sewer, water, etc. The Hoover Institution estimates that unfunded urban pension liabilities alone amount to $3.846 trillion.[127] This compares to total municipal bond debt of $3.7 trillion[128] that certainly must be serviced as a top priority. Both of these figures are unquestionably much larger as of 2018. The combined city infrastructure deficit (deferred maintenance) is estimated between $1.2 and $3.5 trillion, but this is very subjective because no one really knows how many projects could be launched if funds were actually available. U.S. household debt accumulated by citizens who inhabit these same American cities has risen to over $13 trillion.[129] A quick calculation of all this city and personal debt indicates that every man, woman and child wakes up each morning with over $60,000 in liability - and this does not include any county, state or federal debts!

Essentially, cities are completely unable to launch new infrastructure projects being sold by Smart City hucksters. So, if funding cannot come from the cities themselves, where is it coming from? Capital investments.

127 Joshua Rauh, Hidden Debt, Hidden Deficits: 2017 Edition, Hoover Institution, May 2017, p. 1.
128 Report on the Municipal Securities Market, Securities and Exchange Commission, July 31, 2012, p 1.
129 *Forbes*, "U.S. Household Debt Reaches Record $13 Trillion", Friedman, Nov. 14, 2017.

Public-Private Partnerships

Shortly after the United Nations passed Resolution 3201, Declaration on the Establishment of a New International Economic Order in 1974, public-private partnerships (PPP) were introduced as a way to finance the development of the new order. It would involve private corporations putting up cash in return for government favors with the result being a sort of Fascist bonding of industry and government. The government favors could be in the form of free tracts of land, tax breaks, special zoning considerations, waivers of regulations, exclusive rights to development, etc. The net result of any public-private partnership is loss of city autonomy and sovereignty and loss of citizens' rights to determine their own future.

Even the United Nations exposed this criticism in one of its own papers:

> *Whitfield (2010) provided a survey of PPPs around the world, showing how the model has been adapted to the economic, political and legal environments of different countries in Europe, North America, Australia, Russia, China, India and Brazil. It also examined the growing secondary market in PPP investments, "buying and selling schools and hospitals like commodities in a global supermarket" (p. 183) as well as the increasing number of PPP failures, usually as a result of investors' "miscalculations; states pick up the tab when they walk away". It found cases of deceptive techniques of assessing value for money (VfM) and manipulations of risk transfer so that PPPs appear to out-perform traditional public provision.* **Most importantly, Whitfield claimed that PPPs undermine democracy by systematically reducing the responsibility, capability, and power of the state.**[130] [emphasis added]

Nevertheless, the document builds a solid case in favor of PPP and in its conclusion, points to the international guidelines for

---

130 *DESA Working Paper No. 148*, "Public-Private Partnerships and the 2030 Agenda for Sustainable Development: Fit for purpose?", Sharma, Platz et. al., Feb. 2006, p. 3.

PPPs contained in the UN's Financing For Development outcome called the *Addis Ababa Action Agenda*:

> *We will therefore build capacity to enter into public-private partnerships, including with regard to planning, contract negotiation, management, accounting and budgeting for contingent liabilities. We also commit to holding inclusive, open and transparent discussion when developing and adopting guidelines and documentation for the use of public-private partnerships, and to build a knowledge base and share lessons learned through regional and global forums.*

The full-court press to implement PPPs throughout America is gaining steam. In 2015, the Department of Transportation unveiled the Build America Transportation Investment Center (BATIC) with the main purpose to cultivate PPPs, helping them to gain access to federal credit and to navigate federal permitting and procedural requirements. Later in 2015, Congress passed the Fixing America's Surface Transportation Act (FAST) that facilitates PPP engagement. Carrying into the current Administration, Secretary of Transportation Elaine Chao stated during her confirmation hearing, "The government does not have the resources to address all the infrastructure needs within our country." She noted that there is a "significant difference between traditional program funding and other innovative financing tools, such as public-private partnerships."[131]

> *In conclusion, when a city commits to converting to a Smart City and PPP deals flow in to finance it, there are only two possible outcomes. First, if a project demonstrably fails, the private investor will leave the deal and the city will suffer through the resulting wreckage and hubris. The other outcome is that the private entity will end up controlling the city like a puppet on a string. In the meantime, the city will be 'transformed' with failed urban planning techniques from the 1950s and 1960s. As you can see, there is no way for a city to exit in better shape than when it entered.*

---

131 *Washington Post*, "Elaine Chao emphasizes private funds for Trump's promised transportation fixes", January 11, 2017.

Smart Regions

To globalist Smart City planners, multiple cities bordering each other are seen as a city-region. These metro-areas are often referred to as such: Phoenix metro, the Bay Area, Los Angeles area, and so on. These regions present a huge problem to Technocrat planners because each city has its own degree of sovereignty as well as an independent city council. Some cities are fiercely independent and simply won't go along with what neighboring cities want to do. In the age of complex technology, Smart City solutions demand uniformity and standardized connectivity., and trying to get many cities together on any single issue is like herding feral cats. What's a planner to do?

The answer is to create Smart Regions as a higher layer of governance and simply usurp sovereignty from all cities within the region. This brand new paradigm is already spreading like wildfire.

On October 25, 2018, the *Second Annual Smart Regions Conference* was held in Columbus, Ohio. It was heavily sponsored by companies like Cisco, Intel, Hitachi, Oracle, IEEE, Verizon, American Automobile Association (AAA) and others. The Department of Homeland Security was listed as a government sponsor. Many NGOs and universities were also noted, like the Ohio State University, National Association of Development Organizations (NADO), Venture Smarter and Global Cities Team Challenge.

The conference organizer, Smart Regions Initiative, clearly explains their activities and intentions:

*We believe that communities of all sizes deserve the tools to successfully navigate digital transformation and growth. SRI is dedicated to helping leaders build better places to live, work, and visit by leveraging smart technologies, policies, and strategies to optimize or altogether replace outdated systems and infrastructure, **making government agencies more efficient and effective**.*

*Smart Regions Initiatives educate and engage key stakehold-
ers and community members **to accelerate the development of smart cities and regions in urban, suburban,
and rural areas.** Our team and partners support standards
development to promote interoperability, policy development to support smart planning, and project development to
accelerate success timelines.*[132] [emphasis added]

Note in the first instance the goal of "making government
agencies more efficient and effective." In the second instance, the
means of accomplishing this is to accelerate development of "regions in urban, suburban and rural areas."

One early adopter of this new regional governance paradigm
is seen in the Greater Phoenix Smart Region Initiative, defined
as a public-private nonprofit partnership including Arizona
State University Center for Smart Cities and Regions, the Arizona
Institute for Digital Progress (IDP) and the Greater Phoenix
Economic Council. The target is focused on Maricopa County
where 22 cities and towns and 4.2 million citizens.

ASU, located in Tempe, Arizona, claims to be the number one
university in America for Sustainable Development. IDP was specifically set up to be the implementation partner for Initiative.
ASU and IDP are charged to create the "smart cities digital road
map" containing "a set of regionwide key priorities" that are yet
to be created. Where has IDP received its inspiration? Primarily.
it has...

*looked to other similar public-private partnerships to grow
smart city projects, like the Dallas Innovation Alliance
in Texas, the Internet of Things (IoT) Consortium at the
University of Southern California and the numerous Smart
Kansas City initiatives in Missouri.*[133]

Note that the Greater Phoenix Smart Region Initiative has no
elected representatives and no citizen oversight. Cities are only
included as stakeholders, and they will be lucky if they get to send
one delegate to the meetings. Who gave any of these people the

132 See SmartRegions.org page "About Smart Cities Initiatives".
133 *Government Technology*, "Phoenix Partnership Promises to Further Regional Smart Cities Work",
October 2, 2018.

authority to usurp sovereignty and authority from these cities? No one! When decisions are made for implementing the Smart City solution for the entire region, will individual cities sponsor a referendum for citizens to vote on participation? Or will individual city councils approve the measures by specific vote? Not likely!

Unfortunately, all of these 22 cities are already conditioned to bow to regional governance by the existence of the Maricopa Association of Governments (MAG), which is a Councils of Governments (COGS) entity spanning the same area and population. All of these regional governance schemes are patently unconstitutional and very possibly illegal.

Such is the Smart City steamroller.

CHAPTER 6

BUILDING NETWORKS OF CITIES

*Networks of cities provide a powerful tool for
economic policies of territorial basis proposing
new strategies regarding to the objectives of equity,
sustainability and competitiveness.*[132]

Since most economic activity takes place within cities, it is not surprising that the modern globalization process focuses on urban transformation and control. It follows then that trade between cities depends upon infrastructure and connectivity. This infrastructure must provide two distinct functions in order to be useful to the globalist machine: first, it must be able to service the supply-chain that moves raw materials and value-added components to manufacturing and assembly factories; second, it must be able to deliver finished goods and services to consumers. In today's economy, the inputs for manufacturing and the consumers for finished goods might be found in any part of the world. This is a different scenario to one hundred years earlier where manufacturing plants were generally located in close proximity to the raw materials needed for their production.

The rapidly advancing field of Supply Chain Management (SCM) has done more to advance the cause of globalization than any other factor in the last 50 years. Advances in computers, communication and transportation have been carefully orchestrated to create a finely-tuned and sophisticated network resembling the

---

132 RafaelBoix, Networks of Cities and Growth, Università di Firenze, 2013, p. 34.

circulatory and nervous systems in the human body. Politically speaking, the concept of "infrastructure" is closely associated to SCM. Governments never speak to citizens in terms of improving SCM, but rather in terms of building or rebuilding infrastructure, and this is especially true in America today. The citizenry is led to believe spending tax dollars on infrastructure means fixing the potholes on the Interstate, repairing bridges and overpasses, installing fiber optic Internet cables to their neighborhood, etc. The professionals of globalization see infrastructure in a completely different light: it connects cities together in functional relationships to fit into and service the global supply chain.

Since her January 2017 appointment as Secretary of Transportation, Elaine Chao has consistently championed the Trump Administration's $1 trillion infrastructure rebuilding initiative but has provided a twist: the federal spending shortfall will be made up by the creation of public-private partnerships (P3), commingling private funds with public tax dollars. If the Administration puts up $200 billion to kickstart a $1 trillion infrastructure project, is it even conceivable that the private investors who put up $800 billion will not seek their own requirements instead of the public interest? Not likely.

If P3 were the only issue brought to the infrastructure table by Elaine Chao, it would be troubling enough, but there is a much deeper concern. Chao's father, Dr. James Chao, founded a privately-held global shipping company called Foremost Maritime Corporation in 1964 that now owns at least 27 giant cargo ships. The majority of these are large bulk carriers known as "capesize" vessels dedicated to dry-weight cargo such as coal, iron ore or other commodity raw materials.

In 1958, the elder Chao immigrated from Taiwan to the United States and in 1961 brought his wife and young children, including their firstborn, eight year-old Elaine. While building Foremost over the years, the Chao family has developed and maintained strong ties to the Chinese government. Its most recent ship purchases in 2017, for instance, were made from the state-owned China State Shipping Corporation (CSSC). Elaine's sister Angela

Chao, currently Deputy-Chairman of Foremost and in charge of day-to-day operations, was appointed in January 2017 to the board of directors of the state-owned Bank of China. The Bank of China is the fourth largest bank in the world, easily eclipsing JPMorgan Chase, Bank of America and Wells Fargo & Co. It has branches throughout the world and is a major presence in the United States with Bank of China USA.

Bank of China is fully involved with China's massive infrastructure project called "One Belt One Road" (BRI) which seeks to connect Asia with Europe along the lines of the ancient Silk Road and will include roads, pipelines, seaports and ocean shipping routes. The estimated cost of BRI is well into the trillions,[133] and not surprisingly, Beijing is expecting to couple private investments through the liberal use of Public-Private Partnerships.

With Elaine Chao's sister and father so deeply and directly involved with the Chinese government and its own infrastructure projects, Secretary Chao has a major conflict of interest: will she build America's infrastructure to serve the American citizen, or will she build it according to the desires of the global Technocracy?

That's a bold statement, so I will digress to explain further. China is not only a Technocracy, but it is currently the global leader in exporting Technocracy to all parts of the world. Although it still has the trappings of a Communist dictatorship, it has long since departed from Communism in favor of Technocracy. Few people recognize this because of a general ignorance about Technocracy. However, a 2001 article in *Time Magazine*, "Made in China: Revenge of the Nerds," clearly makes the case:

The nerds are running the show in today's China. In the twenty years since Deng Xiaoping's reforms kicked in, the composition of the Chinese leadership has shifted markedly in favor of technocrats. ...It's no exaggeration to describe the current regime as a technocracy.

After the Maoist madness abated and Deng Xiaoping inaugurated the opening and reforms that began in late 1978, sci-

133 CNBC, "China's plan to develop Asian infrastructure could cost trillions", Evelyn Cheng, 23 June 2017.

entific and technical intellectuals were among the first to be rehabilitated. Realizing that they were the key to the Four Modernizations embraced by the reformers, concerted efforts were made to bring the "experts" back into the fold.

During the 1980s, technocracy as a concept was much talked about, especially in the context of so-called "Neo-Authoritarianism"*— the principle at the heart of the "Asian Developmental Model" that South Korea, Singapore, and Taiwan had pursued with apparent success. The basic beliefs and assumptions of the technocrats were laid out quite plainly:* ***Social and economic problems were akin to engineering problems and could be understood, addressed, and eventually solved as such.***[134][emphasis added]

How did China arrive at this position? China was originally brought onto the global economic stage by prominent members of the Trilateral Commission during the Carter presidency from 1976-1980. With an assist from Trilateral Henry Kissinger, it was primarily Trilateral Zbigniew Brzeziński who received the bulk of credit; but, we must remember that both Jimmy Carter and his Vice-President Walter Mondale, were also Commission members, as was Secretary of State Cyrus Vance. After China's introduction to the West, it was smothered with Western capital, infrastructure projects, factories and most importantly, knowhow and instruction on Technocracy. Deng Xiaoping's reforms discussed above were the result of those original Trilateral discussions. It took only 23 years for the *Time Magazine* article to articulate the result.

Today, China is a fully-engineered and technocrat-run society that continues to expand its infrastructure in order to achieve economic and trade domination. This is what *One Belt One Road* is all about: perfecting the supply chain of goods and services between China and Europe. To sell the effort, China has become the top supporter of the UN's 2030 Agenda for Sustainable Development. When Chinese President Xi Jinping addressed the Belt and Road Forum in May 2017 he stated,

---

134 *Time Magazine*, "Made in China: Revenge of the Nerds", Kaiser Kuo, June 2001.

We should pursue the new vision of green development and a way of life and work that is green, low-carbon, circular and sustainable. Efforts should be made to strengthen cooperation in ecological and environmental protection and build a sound ecosystem so as to realise the goals set by the 2030 Agenda for Sustainable Development... We will set up a big data service platform on ecological and environmental protection. We propose the establishment of an international coalition for green development on the Belt and Road, and we will provide support to related countries in adapting to climate change.[135]

Connecting the dots on the above, we find that,

- Elaine Chao is Secretary of Transportation in charge of developing U.S. infrastructure
- Her father is heavily involved in global infrastructure as head of a major shipping company, Foremost Group, and has close ties with the Chinese government and its top leadership, all of whom are steeped in Technocracy
- Her younger sister Angela is a director of the state-owned Bank of China, the fourth largest bank in the world and senior financier to China's One Belt One Road infrastructure initiative.

There is also one other small problem: Elaine Chao is married to Senate Majority Leader Mitch McConnell which means she has a direct conduit into the legislative apparatus of Congress.

Besides her connections to China, Secretary Chou has other P3 allies to finance infrastructure projects. The World Bank has widely promoted P3s to the world, in spite of many calling it a failed model:

This week, executive directors of the World Bank were handed a letter signed by more than 80 civil society organizations and trade unions from around the world, urging a change in the bank's approach to public-private partnerships.

---

135 *Scroll.in*, "As China eyes global clout with Belt and Road Initiative, what price will the environment pay?", Giovanni Ortolani, May 30, 2018.

*This action, during the IMF and World Bank Group Spring Meetings, should not have come as a surprise. It is part of a global campaign on PPPs launched last October with the support of more than 150 organizations that are exasperated by the lack of action on this critical issue. The campaign manifesto outlines CSOs' alarm at the **increasing promotion of PPPs to deliver infrastructure projects and public services around the world, and in particular the World Bank's role in energetically promoting these contracts.**[136]* [emphasis added]

It is important for the reader to understand how the World Bank has been one of the chief promoters of globalization over the past 40 years. Working with the International Monetary Fund (IMF) and the Bank for International Settlements (BIS), the World Bank has brokered thousands of deals between private firms and government entities, many of which have ended in utter disaster. However, their failures have never deterred them from continuing the practice.

As far as America's future infrastructure is concerned, Elaine Chou is siding with globalization in general and the World Bank in particular. One must ask the question, how can this possibly turn out to serve the interests of the American people instead of those promoting globalization? Of course, it can't. Supply chain considerations will always be first in such an arrangement, and when a deal goes sour with the private party exiting the partnership, the civic entity will be left high-and-dry with the hubris.

It is also important for the reader to understand that Public-Private Partnerships are considered essential by the United Nations to implement its seventeen Sustainable Development Goals that are part of the 2030 Agenda adopted by the UN on September 25, 2015. The connection between P3s and SDGs has been stated and restated by many UN agencies, but it has also been parotted in American media as well:

Public Private Partnerships, (PPPs), which are a controversial source of funding for government projects, are back at

---

136 Maria Romero, "Public-private partnerships don't work", Devex, 19 April 2018.

the current World Bank IMF meetings in Washington, under a new name — Blended Finance. **Proponents say that blended finance is a way to fund the $2.5 trillion a year needed to "support progress towards the Sustainable Development Goals (SDGs) set forth by the United Nations."**[137] [emphasis added]

Devolution of Nation-States

The most powerful political impulse propelling us toward a connected world is precisely the one that points in the opposite direction: *devolution.* Devolution is the perpetual fragmentation of territory into ever more (and smaller) units of authority, from empires to nations, nations to provinces, and provinces to cities. Devolution is the ultimate expression of the tribal, local, and parochial desire to control one's geography which is exactly why it drives us toward a connected destiny.[138]

Global technocrat and scholar Dr. Parag Khanna is revered by the global elite as an open advocate for Technocracy. If they listen to him, which they do, then we should listen to him as well. One of Khanna's favorite topics of discussion is devolution. *"The 21st century's strongest political force is not democracy but devolution,"* he wrote in a 2014 article titled *Dismantling Empires Through Devolution.*[139] He went on to write,

Devolution—meaning the decentralization of power—is the geopolitical equivalent of the second law of thermodynamics: inexorable, universal entropy. Today's nationalism and tribalism across Europe, Africa, and the Middle East represent the continued push for either greater autonomy within states or total independence from what some view as legacy colonial structures. Whether these movements are for devolution,

---

137 *Forbes*, "'Blended Finance' -- Lipstick On The Public-Private Partnership Pig?", Tom Groenfeldt, April 20, 2018.
138 Khanna, Parag, *Connectography: Mapping the Future of Global Civilization* (Kindle Locations 1375-1378). Random House Publishing Group. Kindle Edition.
139 *The Atlantic*, "Dismantling Empires Through Devolution", Parag Khanna, Sept. 26, 2014.

federalism, or secession, they all to varying degrees advocate the same thing: greater self-rule.[140]

There are often counter intuitive twists and turns in understanding Technocracy, and devolution is one of them. Promoting "greater self-rule" in local areas accomplishes two key goals for Technocracy. First, autonomous cities are more easily enticed into connecting to the global supply chain. Second, large democratic structures that would resist Technocracy, whether overtly or by bureaucratic red-tape, are more easily restructured to provide the system under which the general society can be re-engineered. In other words, the little problems and details of local governance don't matter to Technocrats as long as they are in charge of creating the master system under which they all operate.

This is exactly what has happened in China over the last 40 years, leading many technocrat-minded leaders in the free-world to praise the "China model" of governance over the American model. Parag Khanna minced no words when he stated, "China, the most populous empire in history, is trying to reorganize itself into a collection of two dozen urban technocratic hubs. America should do the same."[141]

The Chinese government provides hard and fast rules and policies (the engineering) that all citizens must follow, but how they choose to follow in their local communities is up to the local citizens. The *tools of Technocracy* are devised and provided from the top level, but their use is carried out by local communities. Khanna points to this with statements like,

> *American democracy could be made far more effective through **the technocratic toolkit** being deployed around the world in better-run countries. There are three things that the best governments do well: Respond efficiently to citizens' needs and preferences, learn from international experience in devising policies, and **use data and scenarios for long-term planning.** If done right, such governments marry the virtues of democratic inclusiveness with the effectiveness of*

---

140 Ibid.

141 *Technocracy in America*, Parag Khanna, Createspace, 2017, p. 52.

technocratic management. **The ideal type of government that results is what I call a direct technocracy.** [142] [emphasis added]

What kind of things are in this *technocratic toolkit?* In China's case, it is easy to pick out key components:

- National funding for high-tech projects like 5G, Internet of Things (IoT), Smart Grid infrastructure, high speed trains, advanced surveillance cameras and sensors, etc.
- Physical infrastructure to connect cities and regions
- Architecture for Smart City construction
- Trade infrastructure such as One Belt, One Road
- Artificial Intelligence, supercomputer capacity
- The legal framework for Public-Private Partnerships
- Foreign policy and trade agreements

Trying to merge "technocratic management" with "democratic inclusiveness" is an oxymoron on one hand, but it shows how Technocracy intends to handle citizen representation. Communities can vote on how the trash should be collected or which side of the road the bicycle lane is on, but all other decisions are left up to the technocrats.

Devolution in America got underway in 1993 with the inauguration of President William Jefferson Clinton and Vice President Albert Gore, both former members of the elite Trilateral Commission. Clinton signed Executive Order 12862 on September 11, 1993 that formalized the National Performance Review (NPR) headed by Gore. NPR was later renamed the National Partnership for Reinventing Government. NPR was inspired by a book published in early 1993, *Reinventing Government* by David Osborne and Ted Gaebler. A book review published just three months later provided insight into where this was headed:

In Reinventing Government, David Osborne and Ted Gaebler attempt to chart a course between big government and laissez faire. They want nothing to do with "ideology." Rather **Osborne and Gaebler are technocrats in search of prag-**

---

matic answers. *"Reinventing Government," they write, "addresses how governments work, not what governments do." Thus, from the standpoint of what governments do, the book is a proverbial grab bag of policy prescriptions, some good, some bad.*[143] [Emphasis added]

In fact, Vice President Al Gore chose Osborne to be his senior advisor in running the NPR.

In 1999, Clinton's program was so impressive that it was recognized by the United Nations as a global program under the auspices of the U.N. Public Administration Programme (UNPAP) which stated:

> *The Global Forum was first organized by the Government of the United States in 1999. Since then, it has emerged as one of the most significant global events to address government reinvention. Subsequent forums have been organized by the Governments of Brazil, Italy, Morocco, Mexico and the Republic of Korea, respectively. During the 6th Global Forum held in Seoul in May 2005, the United Nations Under-Secretary General invited participants to the 7th Global Forum to be held at the UN Headquarters.*[144]

Essentially, the goal of reinventing government was to convert from a bureaucratic to a business model of governance. This shifted the mission of government to treat citizens like customers while answering to corporate stakeholders instead.[145] Running government like a corporation permits the natural devolution of authority to spread to states, regions and most importantly, cities. In place of centralized authority, regulations replaced unified law and all of the resulting entities were "empowered" to do whatever it took to get the corporate mission accomplished.

This is not easily seen or understood without an example. The most egregious illustration is the nationwide blanket of regional Councils of Governments that has been thoroughly co-opted by the "reinvented government." The National Association of

143 *Freeman*, "Reinventing Government", Franklin Harris, Jr., May 1, 1993.
144 UN Public Administration Programme, *The Global Forum on Reinventing Government.*
145 Wood, Patrick, *Technocracy Rising: The Trojan Horse of Global Transformation*, Coherent Publishing, 2017, p. 105.

Regional Councils (NARC) oversees state Councils which in turn oversee local Councils. NARC provides its own history:

> *The National Association of Regional Councils (NARC), then called the National Service to Regional Councils (NSRC), was created in 1965 by the National League of Cities and the National Association of Counties to respond to the professional and legislative needs of America's emerging, multipurpose, multi-jurisdictional organizations of local governments. By 1967, the more than 350 Regional Councils in the country were at the forefront of forging regional alliances for the purpose of addressing common, multi-jurisdictional challenges. These organizations are known as regional planning agencies, development districts and councils of governments, among other names. It was in 1967 that NARC became an independent entity for regions.*
>
> **Today, Regional Councils have retained their identity but their role has changed dramatically. Of the more than 500 Regional Councils throughout the country,** *some include Metropolitan Planning Organizations (MPO).* **More than 400 MPOs have been established to serve as urban regional transportation entities in areas with a population of 50,000 or more. Some MPOs are extensions of Regional Councils, and slightly more than half are stand-alone organizations responsible for fulfilling federal and state metropolitan transportation planning requirements.** *A board of elected officials and other community leaders typically governs each Regional Council and MPO.*
>
> *NARC supports its membership by advocating and representing their interests on national issues, with the U.S. Congress and the Executive Branch. The function of the Regional Council and the MPO has been shaped by changing dynamics in federal, state and local government relations, and **the recognition that the region is the arena in which local governments must work together to address challenges – social, economic, workforce, transportation, emergency preparedness, environmental and others.*** *Additionally,*

Regional Councils and MPOs are often called upon to deliver various federal, state programs that require a regional approach, such as, transportation or comprehensive planning, services for the elderly and clearinghouse functions.

Regional Councils and MPOs have learned to be entrepreneurial *due to shifts in priorities for federal funds. These organizations are experienced collaborators, adept at bringing people together and getting results.* **States are relying more on these organizations as vehicles for engaging local governments and delivery of programs.**[146] [emphasis added]

The 400 Metropolitan Planning Organizations (MPOs) administer transportation regulations and Federal/state funding to the local cities (think infrastructure, connectivity). This funding used to go directly to the cities, but now it has been intercepted by the MPOs in order to enforce and advance their own "sustainable" agenda. They are not run by locally elected civic representatives, and no individual city or county would dare to resist for fear of losing Federal infrastructure funding.

Note that Councils of Governments also assert authority over regional planning, land use, zoning and property rights policies in their respective "regions", while usurping or overriding duly elected city and county representatives.

Some might say that coordination and cooperation is a good thing, and others might even agree. The real problem with Councils of Governments is that they are patently and outrageously unConstitutional from top to bottom! Article 4, Section 4 of the Constitution states: **"The United States shall guarantee to every State in this Union a Republican Form of Government."** What is a Republic form of Government? It is defined as **"a government in which supreme power is held by the citizens entitled to vote and is exercised by elected officers and representatives governing according to law."**

---

146 Narc.org/about-narc/about-the-association/history

Thus, the reinvented Federal government has devolved by distributing jurisdiction to regional Councils of Government, rather than to citizens directly.

It is noteworthy that COGs and MPOs are not government organizations at all. They have no direct taxation power, no regulatory authority and no police powers. They never hold elections for any position and membership is said to be voluntary. If they have no "teeth", then how can they wield so much influence over an entire region? The answer is money.

Here is an odd mix of public-private partnership where the COG/MPO partners with the Federal Department of Transportation to act as a middleman for Federal funds. For instance, President Obama signed the Fixing America's Surface Transportation (FAST) act on December 4, 2015. FAST authorized $305 billion over fiscal years 2016 through 2020 for highway construction, public transportation and railroad improvements, among other related things.

According to the Federal Highway Administration (FHA), the FAST Act authorizes each state to receive a lump sum of money representing the sum of its projects, except the state does not actually receive the money. The FHA rules specifically state, "funding is set aside for the State's Metropolitan Planning program..." The MPO/COG is then free to dangle the funds over their cities and counties to force them to comply with their UN-driven Sustainable Development and 2030 Agenda programs.

Conclusion

America's infrastructure is being built out by Technocrats according to a narrow focus on furthering Sustainable Development via infrastructure and Supply Chain Management. If there are benefits for American citizens, they will be incidental to the greater cause. Government actors are wrought with conflicts of interest, and their means of delivery (COGs, MPOs) are unConstitutional.

The overall purpose of connecting the world's cities into a global network is to further implement the UN's Sustainable

Development policies, the 17 Sustainable Development Goals and 2030 Agenda. This was made abundantly clear in Khanna's book *Connectography*:

> The World Bank argues that **infrastructure is the "missing link"** in achieving the Millennium Development Goals related to poverty, health, education, and other objectives, and infrastructure has been formally included in the latest Sustainable Development Goals ratified in 2015.[147] [emphasis added]

147 Khanna, Parag. *Connectography: Mapping the Future of Global Civilization* (Kindle Locations 528-530). Random House Publishing Group. Kindle Edition.

CHAPTER 7

GLOBALIST TOOLS OF DEVOLUTION

Be not intimidated... nor suffer yourselves to be whee-
dled out of your liberties by any pretense of politeness,
delicacy, or decency. These are but three different names
for hypocrisy, chicanery and cowardice. - John Adams
(1765)

The global elite have always been less tight-lipped about
their globalist strategies than their tools designed to
achieve them. After all, if someone threatened to murder you,
there wouldn't be too much you could do unless you knew how
they were going to do it. Knowing how would let you build a defense against your attacker. This principle is not lost on the agents
of transformation.

This chapter will examine three of the more prominent tools of
devolution that are being used to flip America into Technocracy.
These tools are thoroughly described by academia and policy
makers but are largely unknown to the public. This fact has made
it virtually impossible for activists and critics to gain any momentum in resisting the implementation of things like Sustainable

Development, Agenda 21, 2030 Agenda, New Urban Agenda and Green Economy, to name a few.

Reflexive law

Chapter 7 of *Technocracy Rising: The Trojan Horse of Global Transformation* first described the theory and practice of Reflexive Law in America and to my knowledge, offered the first modern critical analysis.

It is well-known that the U.S. Constitution is based on the Rule of Law. In fact, the front of the beautiful Supreme Court building in Washington, D.C. is engraved with "EQUAL JUSTICE UNDER LAW". This is a wonderful concept that codified well-published laws that would apply to every citizen in exactly the same way regardless of race, religion, sex or national origin.. In fact, the phrase, "nobody is above the law", is legendary in America.

The Constitution provides that laws are made only by Congress which is made up of broadly elected representatives of the people. The Executive branch enforces these laws, and the Supreme Court insures that they are not contrary to the Constitution. This system of checks and balances is seen nowhere else on planet earth. It is at the very core of what made America into the greatest nation in history. Unfortunately, this is not the case today.

Perpetrators of Sustainable Development found early on that they could make no headway in America under the traditional Rule of Law. One environmental law journal writing about Reflexive Law succinctly described the problem:

...sustainable development's broad sweep strains our intellectual grasp of its meaning and outruns the capacity of our current legal and political systems to channel society's activities toward its achievement... there is no doubt that sustainable development needs new paradigms to transform it from visionary rhetoric to a viable political goal. [151]

---

151 Gaines, "Reflexive Law as a Legal Paradigm for Sustainable Development", *Buffalo Environmental Law Journal*, (2002).

Apparently, Sustainable Development was merely "visionary rhetoric" until Reflexive Law came to the table. In this case, it is very clear that the intention of this new system would drive political and societal change outside of Constitutional authority or restrictions. In addition, the "capacity of our current legal and political systems" was inadequate to contain the scope and intent of Sustainable Development; this is an understatement, however, because if left to itself to work as originally intended, our legal and political system would have rejected and banished it on sight.

Reflexive Law originated with a German legal scholar, Gunther Teubner, in 1982. It was described clearly in 2001:

> Reflexive describes "an action that is directed back upon it-self:. For the purposes of Systems Theory reflexivity is defined as the application of a process to itself, e.g., "thinking of thinking", "communicating about communication: "teaching how to teach", etc. In the context of law reflexivity could be "making laws on law-making, "adjudicating on adjudication", or "regulating self-regulation". It is obvious, that **the focus of Reflexive Law in this context is rather on procedure than on substantive law.**[152] [emphasis added]

A foundational concept of Technocracy is Systems Theory which is based on the idea that systems can be self-regulating by using continuous feedback of the system itself. Systems Theory is applied to all kinds of disciplines such as psychology, sociology, ecology and business. It is a core tenet of artificial intelligence (AI) where algorithms teach themselves new behavior based on new learning experiences or changing conditions. The law journal goes on to state:

> Another meaning of reflexive is **"marked by or capable of reflection"**, referring to reflexion in its philosophical meaning of "introspective contemplation or consideration of some subject matter". Here one can find the normative implications of Reflexive Law as being connected with a concept of ratio-nality. However, rationality is not understood as a quality of norms, but in accordance with **Discourse Theory** rather as

---
152 Graif-Peter Calliess, "Lex Mercatoria: A Reflexive Law Guide To An Autonomous Legal System", *German Law Journal*, (2001).

*communicative rationality. In a nutshell, **decision-making
in a reflexive legal system shall be marked by thorough
deliberation or reasoning as well as by reflection on the
specific function and limits of law in modern society.**
Teubner suggests that such reflection would lead to a non-
interventionist model of the State and of Law the latter of
which is essentially limits itself to what we can call **the con-
stitutionalisation of self-regulation.**[153]* [emphasis added]

We learn here that Reflexive Law is not rational in the traditional sense, but only in accordance with Discourse Theory.
The Frenchman Michel Foucault (1925-1984) was the father of
Discourse Theory which states that what society holds to be true
changes over time and is discovered by interaction with members
of society itself. In other words, bring all your facts and studies
to the table and then debate them until a consensus is reached.
The push and shove of stakeholders (those with pertinent information related to the discussion) is ultimately dominated by the
more powerful, persuasive or clever ones.

Thus, Reflexive Law is an irrational legal system based on current and changing societal norms, using itself to determine legal
outcomes. If this turns your mind into a pretzel, don't be alarmed;
take a deep breath and then read from the beginning again.

Now, let me give you some context. The title of the above paper is "Lex Mercatoria", which is Latin for *Merchant Law* that was
prevalent in Europe during the medieval period. It was a system
of custom and best practices that decided cases *ex aequo et bono,*
or simply put, by arbitration. It dispensed with legal technicalities
of respective nations or districts. Arbitration is not an uncommon
practice today, but it requires the specific consent of both parties before negotiations begin. Arguments and discussions are
factored in to arrive at a fair "ruling" and then the case is closed.
What happens in one arbitration case might have a radically different outcome in another because it is subject to the whims of
the jurists. Obviously, this is not the traditional American "'Rule

153 ibid.

of Law", but be careful not to mistake Reflexive Law for Case Law or Administrative Law. It is altogether different.

Reflexive Law is the primary reason that entire industries have clamored to be deregulated over the past 40 years. Such industries demanded self-regulation and shunned government oversight that could hold them accountable to existing laws and statutes. This would not be evident unless one understood what Reflexive Law is in the first place.

Virtually every lawsuit brought by radical environmental groups against ranchers, farmers, cities, counties, landowners and even states, has been prosecuted according to Reflexive Law. The defendants seldom win a case because they apply a defense according to the Rule of Law, which is a completely different legal theory. In every case, the plaintiffs trot out scientific studies, stakeholders, expert witnesses and computer models, arguing that the environment has suffered irreparable damage caused by the defendant's actual or predicted actions. If these same cases had been prosecuted according to the traditional Rule of Law, the defendants would have consistently prevailed. To put it another way, the environmental plaintiffs play chess while the defendants play checkers. As I wrote in *Technocracy Rising*,

> The problem with Reflexive Law is that it cannot operate in a vacuum, as is suggested, but is at all times subject to those who control it. It is ripe for manipulation. Reflexive Law practitioners can thus direct the discourse, the outcome, and the rule-making in a very real sense like the old West vigilante concept of the local self-appointed sheriff being "judge, jury and executioner."

Collaborative Governance

Collaborative Governance is a defined practice that has existed since the late 1980s, and has spread its influence into every state in the U.S. As you will see, it is closely related and complementary to Reflexive Law and Regional Government. Furthermore, it has been a prime mover in the implementation of Sustainable Development.

The most authoritative definition of Collaborative Governance is:

> *A governing arrangement where one or more public agencies engage non-state stakeholders in a collective decision-making process that is formal, consensus-oriented, and deliberative and that aims to make or implement public policy or manage public programs or assets.*[154]

There are six important criteria that must be noted in this definition:

1. The forum must be initiated by a public agency

2. There must be non-state actors or stakeholders

3. Participants must be involved directly in decision-making

4. Participants meet collectively

5. Decision-making is done by consensus

6. The object is to make or implement binding public policy[155]

The public agencies can be at the federal, state or local level and can be initiated by any type of governmental body. Stakeholders invited may include citizens, non-governmental organizations (NGOs) such as environmental groups, experts, other government agencies and corporations. Again, it is important to remember that stakeholders must be directly engaged in decision-making rather than just serving in a consulting capacity.

The problem with Collaborative Governance is that it is not Constitutional on any level. Allowing non-governmental stakeholders to enter into the decision-making process for public policy completely circumvents the concept of representative government. Yet, the practice is so widespread that the University of Arizona now offers a graduate certificate in Collaborative Governance through its *College of Social & Behavioral Sciences School of Government & Public Policy*. Department literature indi-

154 "Collaborative Governance in Theory and Practice", Journal of Public Administration Research and Theory, Ansell & Gash, (Oxford University Press, 2007).
155 Ibid.

cates that a Masters of Public Administration (MPA) will soon be offered.[156]

The other-worldly nature of Collaborative Governance is clearly seen across academic literature. It is not hidden but bluntly states that it is specifically designed to work outside of traditional representative government:

> *A final lesson suggested by these cases is that even when collaborative practice is done correctly and in an appropriate situation, changing traditional governance is still a daunting task. As Machiavelli observed centuries ago, 'It ought to be remembered that there is nothing more difficult to take in hand, more perilous to conduct, or more uncertain in its success, than to take the lead in the introduction of a new order of things.[157]*

One nest of Collaborative Governance is found in the state of Oregon. On December 16, 2011, the governor of Oregon signed Executive Order 11-12 that formalized Collaborative Governance in the state. It states in part,

> *ESTABLISHING THE OREGON SOLUTIONS NETWORK AND CONNECTING THE WORK OF THE REGIONAL SOLUTIONS CENTERS, OREGON SOLUTIONS AND THE OREGON CONSENSUS PROGRAM*
>
> **Oregon has been a leader in the development of collaborative governance systems and models.** *The state has benefitted from the work of organizations formed to bring together the public, private and civic sectors to solve problems and seize opportunities in a collaborative way.*
>
> *In order to create a prosperous economy, healthy environment and equitable society, a need exists in the state to create an infrastructure to support communities of place and interest that want to take a collaborative approach to solving problems and maximizing opportunities at the state, regional and local level. **A collaborative infrastructure includes resources to support collaborative decision making;***

156 See https://collaborativegovernance.arizona.edu/quick-facts for more information.
157 National Civic Review, "Collaborative Governance Practices and Democracy", David E. Booher, February 23, 2005, p. 32-46.

dispute resolution; implementation; public engagement and interagency cooperation.[158] [emphasis added]

The *Oregon Solutions Program* is housed in the College of Urban and Public Affairs at Portland State University[159], and its Mission Statement is crystal clear:

The mission of Oregon Solutions is to develop sustainable solutions to community-based problems that support economic, environmental, and community objectives and are built through the collaborative efforts of businesses, government and non-profit organizations.[160]

Some of the current projects in progress at the time of this writing include:

- Oregon Sustainability Board, Sustainable Schools Project
- Stream Restoration Partnership
- Renewable Energy and Eastern Oregon Landscape Conservation Partnership
- Transportation Electrification Executive Council
- Southern Oregon Clean Energy Alliance
- Oregon Sustainable Agriculture Resource Center

One might imagine that some participants could become hostile toward decisions that are not seen as in their best interest. In such cases, Oregon Solutions states that "we refer projects of a highly contentious nature to Oregon Consensus, our sister program, and the state's official dispute resolution program."[161] This takes Collaboration projects to the next level of mediation and creates binding solutions from which there is no escape or appeal process.

As an example, Collaborative Governance has been applied in Klamath Falls, Oregon by the Klamath Basin Restoration Agreement (KBRA). KBRA, along with the Klamath River Renewal

158 See original document at the State of Oregon website. https://www.oregon.gov/gov/Documents/executive_orders/eo_1112.pdf.
159 Note: Because of this, Oregon has been in a state of legal anarchy for at least 8 years, and it is no wonder that Portland has racked up such a bad national reputation for crazy environmental and social justice programs.
160 See website at www.orsolutions.org.
161 See website at http://orsolutions.org/our-process/project-criteria

Corporation (KRRC), have orchestrated the planned destruction of four hydroelectric dams on the Klamath River hoping to promote a larger salmon run. Local counties that called for the original KBRA Collaboration governance panel included Del Norte (CA), Humboldt (CA), Siskiyou (CA) and Klamath (OR), but they were overshadowed by the 24 other invited Stakeholders that included:

- U.S Forest Service
- Oregon Water Resource Board
- California Fish & Game
- Bureau of Reclamation
- Karuk, Klamath, Yurok Tribes
- Klamath Citizens Group
- Friends of the River
- Trout Unlimited
- Institute for Fisheries Resources
- American Rivers
- National Center for Conservation Science & Policy

Collectively, the KBRA was able to create binding laws, rules, regulations and sanctions. It is also notable that several Federal agencies were concurrently part of the collaboration process, permitting cross-agency policies that would not have been possible if the agencies had acted on their own. Despite desperate pleas from local citizens, the managing entity for the dam removal, KRRC, "submitted its plan to the Federal Energy Regulatory Commission, as part of its application to transfer the license for the four dams and remove them."[162]

This entire process has lasted over 10 years and has methodically rolled over all opposition and objections. There has been no legislative oversight and no true public representation. Article 4, Section 4 of the U.S. Constitution states that "The United States shall guarantee to every State in this Union a Republican Form of Government...".

---

162 American Rivers, "Plan released for Klamath River Dam Removal", Amy Kober, June 29, 2018.

KBRA itself was declared legally dead only after three failed attempts to get funding from Congress to clean up the mess that dam removal would have made. Undeterred, the project was handed off to another newly created collaboration called Klamath Hydroelectric Settlement Agreement (KHSA), which created the Klamath River Renewal Corporation (KKRC). The stakeholders of the KHSA are almost identical to the defunct KBRA. The KKRC is charged with actual removal of the 4 Klamath river dams which will proceed as soon as the dam licenses are transferred.

In sum, Collaborative Governance is a scourge to the Constitutional Rule of Law upon which America was built, but it is a key tool for implementation of Sustainable Development.

Do not think that Collaborative Governance is an American phenomenon because it is not. In fact, it is alive and well throughout the entire developed world. For instance, it is reported from an Australian academic journal that "It is clear today that governments across the developed world are preaching the gospel of collaboration... their objectives cannot be achieved without collaboration."[163]

Councils of Governments (Regionalism)

When President William Jefferson Clinton and Vice President Al Gore committed themselves to reinventing government in 1993, the concept of regional government organizations quickly merged with the basic tenets of Sustainable Development and Agenda 21 and began to spread their net over our entire country. Historically, regional coordination councils had already existed for several decades, but they were mostly limited to transportation cooperation and coordination between neighboring cities and counties in the more populated urban areas. Some level of interaction between adjacent civic entities had always been acceptable as long as each entity, through its duly-elected representatives, retained power over its own choices.

---

163 Collaborative Governance: A New Era of Public Policy in Australia?, O'Flynn and Wanna, The Australian National University, 2008, p. xi.

When it was determined that these regional councils could be used as an end run around national sovereignty to implement Sustainable Development and Agenda 21, the concept quickly evolved into a full-blown network of regional government entities that covered the nation. The National Association of Regional Councils (NARC) was established to coordinate and support regional governance; state associations of their own regional organizations were established in all but seven states. Today, NARC notes that

> Regional Councils have retained their identity but **their role has changed dramatically.** Of the more than **500 Regional Councils throughout the country,** some include Metropolitan Planning Organizations (MPO). More than 400 MPOs have been established to serve as urban regional transportation entities in areas with a population of 50,000 or more. Some MPOs are extensions of Regional Councils, and slightly more than half are stand-alone organizations responsible for fulfilling federal and state metropolitan transportation planning requirements. A board of elected officials and other community leaders typically governs each Regional Council and MPO.[164] [emphasis added]

In this context, "Regional Councils" refers to Councils of Governments (COGS) and they are closely related to and intertwined with Metropolitan Planning Organizations (MPO). It is accurate to say that all MPOs are also Councils of Governments because they are similarly structured and only address regional issues. One of the largest COGs in the nation is the Association of Bay Area Governments (ABAG) in the Silicon Valley area of northern California. ABAG asserts jurisdiction over 9 counties containing 100 cities and over 7 million people. Each of these cities has its own city councils. ABAG specifically states that its *"planning and research programs are committed to addressing sustainability, resilience and equity in the region."* Furthermore, it states:

> ABAG builds **collaborative partnerships** with local governments, Bay Area leaders and citizens throughout the region

---

164 See NARC website, History page: http://narc.org/about-narc/about-the-association/history/

*to establish shared goals and create a broader framework to examine economic, social and environmental challenges for the region and future generations. **Collaborative participation** envisioned in these partnerships represents a comprehensive strategy to guide how we want to grow, adapt to change, preserve member communities' unique qualities, and create more vibrant and successful initiatives that maximize **ABAG's regional planning objectives and resources.**[165]* [emphasis added]

The collaborative partnerships are achieved by each city sending a *single* elected representative to be part of the ABAG council. After deliberation with experts, environmentalists, NGOs, lawyers and lobbyists, decisions are made that affect the entire region. The problem with this setup is that none of the city councils of the 100 cities have any say in these policies. This is the nature of regionalism, and it is patently unconstitutional and grossly unfair to the 7 million residents who are almost totally unaware of ABAG's existence.

Furthermore, ABAG's so-called "shared goals" are mostly of its own creation, focused on Sustainable Development and orchestrated to affect "economic, social and environmental challenges."

ABAG reaches into many other key areas of life such as land use policies, housing standards and zoning, water resources, energy acquisition and distribution. Most importantly and shockingly, "ABAG also operates as the state-designated clearinghouse for federal grant applications."[166]

This is huge, because COGs have no government powers like police or law making capacities. Once they grabbed the middleman spot for federal grants to the 100 cities and 9 counties, all of which used to receive such grants directly, ABAG inherited an extortion power that they have learned to use expeditiously: Do what we say or you won't get your federal grant allocations. Thus, the individual cities are forced into participating in radical schemes that they did not vote for or approve.

---

165 ibid.
166 ibid.

Note above that NARC states that there are over 500 COGs and 400 MPOs covering the United States, all with essentially the same agenda to force Sustainable Development, Agenda 21 and other United Nations policies on captive cities and counties. Indeed, COGs have been a key driver to bringing these policies to the U.S., and all have worked carefully with Collaborative Governance and Reflexive Law to achieve it. It's little wonder that so many communities seem to have been turned upside-down in the last 24 years, because they have, and most still have no idea of how it was done.

Case Study: Greater Phoenix Smart Region Initiative

In 2018 several non-governmental organizations got together and decided to imprint Smart City planning and technology across the entire greater Phoenix region composed of 30 cities and 4.7 million citizens. It is described as a public-private collaborative partnership and the major participants are Arizona State University Center for Smart Cities and Regions, the Arizona Institute for Digital Progress and the Greater Phoenix Economic Council. The head of the latter group, Chris Camacho, stated:

> Yes, we're somewhat late to the game compared to some other places, but no one has done it in such a large scale with a **collaborative effort** like we're doing. We expect to execute this plan over the next 12 months and it will bring the most significant economic shift this market has seen in decades.[167]
> [emphasis added]

Blending P3 with Collaborative Governance (P3C) is a relatively new concept but is easy enough to understand. A traditional P3 is typically a business deal between a single civic entity and a limited number of commercial entities; contracts are created and signed, rules are put in place and the work begins. A P3 Collaborative Governance brings in as many "stakeholders" as are

---

167 AZBigMedia, "Is Arizona falling behind on the smart cities movement"", Serena Zhang, April 25, 2018.

necessary to make decisions, determine strategies and policies, etc. The actual outcome of a P3C may not be known until late in the game as final decisions are made and agreements are signed.

Smart Region theory and practice is global in scope with new collaborations popping up on every continent. For instance, the Smart City Association in Italy published a paper called "Smart Regions: Paving the Way for Successful Digitalization Strategies Beyond Smart Cities." They are watching the Greater Phoenix Smart Region Initiative like a hawk:

> *For example, in the Greater Phoenix region, the Institute of Digital Progress (iDP) has coordinated the collaboration of multiple municipalities & authorities, as well as private sector partners – including Uber, Intel and Cisco, further supported by the Arizona State University – to address mobility and traffic congestions collectively – winning a multi-million dollar Advanced Transportation And Congestion Management Technologies Deployment (ATCMTD) grant in the process.[168]*

It is not insignificant that one of the co-authors of this paper is Dominic Papa, also a co-founder of the Arizona Institute for Digital Progress. This foreign paper makes their intent perfectly clear and American readers should pay attention:

> *Many cities around the world benefit from innovation and digitization strategies. 'Smart Cities' initiatives provide the catalyst for urban communities to become more resilient and sustainable, affording economic efficiencies, environmental innovations, enhanced public security, smarter mobility, fresh economic activity and 21st century jobs...*

> *As we collectively enter a next chapter of digital evolution,* **we must leave no person behind. Smart region strategies help us achieve that goal.**[169] [emphasis added]

All of these concepts are straight out of the United Nations playbook for Sustainable Development: resilient, sustainable, economic efficiencies, smarter mobility enhanced public security, 21st century jobs and "leave no person behind."

---

168 The Smart City Association, "Smart Regions: Paving the Way for Successful Digitalization Strategies beyond Smart Cities", Boorsma, et al., March 24, 2018.
169 Ibid.

Unfortunately, all of these legal schemes are completely un-known to American citizens; the legal community is in the dark as well. Because devolution of centralized government is necessary for Technocracy and Sustainable Development to take root, it is imperative that Americans understand their methods and tools.

CHAPTER 8

FINTECH: CRYPTO, CASHLESS AND GREEN

Under a scientific dictatorship education will really work -- with the result that most men and women will grow up to love their servitude and will never dream of revolution. There seems to be no good reason why a thoroughly scientific dictatorship should ever be overthrown[172]. - Aldous Huxley

Fintech is more than just an innocuous contraction of "Financial" and "Technology". When 195 nations of the world rubber-stamped the United Nations' 2030 Agenda in 2016, it was widely noted that in order to achieve the 17 Sustainable Development Goals (SDGs), a new financial system would be necessary to reset the global economic system. This is made clear by a leading Fintech news journal:

> *But this change [implementing SDGs] depends in part on a* **reset of the global financial system to ensure that private capital is redeployed to finance the transition to an inclusive, green economy.** *It requires reforming incumbent finance and democratizing such services to drive this global*

172 Huxley, Aldous, *Brave New World Revisited*, New York: Harper & Brothers, 1958.

transition toward accessible green technologies, jobs and in-frastructure.[173] [emphasis added]

The governor of one Central Bank stated that Fintech offers *"the greatest hope for aligning the world's financial systems with the urgent twin objectives of sustainable development and deepening financial inclusion."*[174] The UN itself is very clear that

The financial system will need to evolve to play its role in financing sustainable development. Billions of people and millions of small businesses lack access to financial services.[175]

The UN describes a "quiet revolution" taking place to merge Sustainable Development into the fabric of the financial system, and that it is being led by those governing the financial system: central banks, financial regulators, stock exchanges and the largest financial actors like global banks and financial consultancies.[176] The magnitude of scale that the UN prescribes is not just global, but stunning as well:

Finance needs to access private capital at scale, *with banking alone managing financial assets of almost US$140 trillion and institutional investors, notably pension funds, managing over US$100 trillion, and capital markets, including bond and equities, exceeding US$100 trillion and US$73 trillion respectively.*[177] [emphasis added]

However, these only represent monetized assets. Non monetized assets include things like forest wealth, estimated to be as large as $270 trillion. While you might be tempted to think this isn't that much money, consider that the Gross Domestic Product (GDP) of the entire planet was only $75.4 trillion in 2016. Fintech not only sets its sights on all the income of the world but on all of the monetized and non-monetized assets as well.

Thus, in this short space we have already learned that Fintech

- Is completely global in scope

173 Fintech Singapore, "Green Finance And How Fintech Can Enable Sustainable Development", May 24, 2017,
174 Ibid.
175 UNEP, "The Financial System We Need: Aligning the Financial System With Sustainable Development", October 2015, Page XIII.
176 Ibid., page XVIII.
177 Ibid., page XXII.

- Is the intended and necessary financial system of Sustainable Development
- Wants to include all citizens of the world, leaving no person behind
- Is funded mostly by private corporations
- Redirects money from "brown" assets to green assets
- Uses advanced technology to transform the system from capitalism to Sustainable Development

When the United Nations speaks of a *"reset of the global financial system"*, it harkens back to UN climate tzar Christiana Figueres' statement in 2015:

This is probably the most difficult task we have ever given ourselves, which is to intentionally transform the economic development model, for the first time in human history.[178]

Figueres was careful to note that this transformation was not an event, but a process "because of the depth of the transformation."[179] Indeed, changing the entire economic system is more than just a transformation: It is a foray into the unknown and the unknowable because it is a full reset of the status quo that has never been attempted in human history.

With this as a backdrop, it is necessary to examine the scope and depth of Fintech and how it is being implemented around the world.

Cryptocurrencies

Just about everyone has heard something about *Bitcoin* in the news, but most of it is quite uninformed. The open-source software for Bitcoin, freely available to the entire world for examination, was originally released in 2009. Bitcoin is considered to be the first so-called "decentralized" cryptocurrency. Transactions are generally anonymous, but their details are recorded in a pack-

178 "Figueres: First time the world economy is transformed intentionally" , United Nations Regional Information Centre For Western Europe, Press release, February 3, 2015.
179 Ibid.

et of data called a "blockchain" and stored in a digital "wallet". Furthermore, the blockchain itself is encrypted.

Bitcoins are "mined" digitally as computers around the world compete to solve complex mathematical equations that are increasingly more difficult as more coins are generated. Bitcoin "miners" have set up computer centers all over the world. Specially designed computers are custom-manufactured costing thousands of dollars each. As faster computer chips become available, many miners must replace all of their computers in order to compete with other newly-established miners. The amount of energy consumed by mining operations is staggering and growing at a geometric rate. One expert calculated that in 2017 global mining operations consumed as much energy as the entire nation of Ireland. Consumption in 2018 was expected to rise to one-half percent of all energy produced on earth![180]

Bitcoin is 100 percent digital. There is no physical "coin" and any printed representation of a coin is merely an artist's idea of what they could look like. Something of a physical nature could be stolen by burglars, but traditional thieves are out of luck with Bitcoin. This gave rise to a new generation of cyber-thieves, or hackers, who have been able to worm their way into computers and steal the contents of Bitcoin wallets. In fact, hundreds of million of dollars worth of Bitcoin have been stolen this way from both individuals and trade exchanges.

Since Bitcoin's inception, over 4,000 other cryptocurrency variations have been programmed and put into play around the world. Reflecting Bitcoin as the founding cryptocurrency, these variants are collectively called "altcoins" even though each has its own name. Some of the more prominent and recognizable altcoins are known as Ethereum, Ripple, Litecoin, Monero, Dogecoin and so on. A few altcoin cryptocurrencies have had limited success, but none as much as Bitcoin.

Nobody knows definitively who created Bitcoin in the first place. The name Satoshi Nakamoto is most often attributed but no one has been able to identify or locate him, leading many in-

---

180 *The Economist*, "Why bitcoin uses so much energy", July 9, 2018.

vestigators to believe that the name is a pseudonym that represents a group rather than a person. Whatever the case, it *has* been carefully documented that Nakamoto's personal ownership of Bitcoins that he mined was worth over $19 billion at the peak of the market in December 2017. The fact that it is hard to conceal this amount of wealth only adds to the mystery surrounding the origin of Bitcoin. Nobody is taking credit for it! Who would not want to be hailed as one of the world's greatest and wealthiest programmers?

The mystery may be partially explained by a white paper published in 1997 by three employees of the National Security Agency (NSA), titled, *How To Make A Mint: The Cryptography Of Anonymous Electronic Cash*. Yes, *that* National Security Agency. It laid out almost all of the major requirements and problems of a cryptographic currency that later turned up in Bitcoin. The point of the paper was "electronic cash" which was "an attempt to construct an electronic payment system modelled after our paper money system".[181]

The NSA's definition of electronic cash is very precise:

The term 'electronic cash' often is applied to any electronic payment scheme that superficially resembles money. In fact, however, electronic cash is a specific kind of electronic payment scheme, defined by certain cryptographic properties.[182]

The paper describes various ways to use public and private cryptographic keys to validate electronic transactions and the need to have an encrypted "electronic wallet" in which to store the electronic coins. Incidentally, throughout the document, electronic cash is referred to as "coin." In fact, the word "coin" appears 188 times just 32 pages of text.

While there is no clear evidence connecting the NSA to the development of Bitcoin, it is clear that it was thinking ahead to the day that such a currency would exist. Is is possible that the release of Bitcoin was a trial balloon to see if consumers would

---

181 (Laurie, Law, Susan Sabett, Jerry, Solinas, (11 January 1997). "How to Make a Mint: The Cryptography of Anonymous Electronic Cash". American University Law Review. 46.
182 Ibid.

willingly accept a digital currency in replacement of cash. If this was the case, the NSA made their point because Bitcoin is now used throughout the world for all kinds of borderless financial transactions. In fact, Bitcoin has developed fanatical and loyal followers who generally believe that it will completely dethrone the existing monetary system of fractional banking, supplanting it with an untraceable, anonymous way to conduct business. Not surprisingly, many of these followers identify as Libertarians and Anarchists.

In the midst of crypto-madness, central banks of the world have been quietly plotting their own strategies to co-opt the distributed blockchain model of cryptocurrencies in favor of a centralized blockchain to be maintained by them. In other words, the details of every cryptocurrency transaction would be flashed back to a centralized database where it would be tracked and analysed ad infinitum.

Bank of England is a case in point. In 2015, BoE created a swat team of high-level computer scientists to determine how it could implement a centralized cryptocurrency. They quickly learned how to do it but stopped their inquiry in early 2018 when they concluded that customers would prefer their currency over others and subsequently close their commercial bank accounts. This could wreak havoc on the financial system. They also concluded that a cryptocurrency would interfere with interest rate policy used to maintain financial stability. BoE reversed field later in 2018 when its governor said he was open-minded about a central-bank-issued digital currency.

The Bank for International Settlements (BIS), which is the central bank to central banks, is based in Basel, Switzerland. The BIS has been looking intently at cryptocurrencies for global banking solutions. While the BIS may not be the originator of any digital currency, it sets policy for its members who might do so. Thus, central bank cryptocurrencies (CBCCs) are a hot topic.

For the U.S., for instance, the BIS touts Fedcoin:

The concept of a retail CBCC has been widely discussed by bloggers, central bankers and academics. Perhaps the most frequently discussed proposal is Fedcoin (Koning (2014, 2016), Motamedi (2014)). As discussed in Box B, the idea is for the Federal Reserve to create a cryptocurrency that is similar to bitcoin. However, unlike with bitcoin, only the Federal Reserve would be able to create Fedcoins and there would be one-for-one convertibility with cash and reserves. Fedcoins would only be created (destroyed) if an equivalent amount of cash or reserves were destroyed (created) at the same time. Like cash, Fedcoin would be decentralised in transaction and centralised in supply. Sveriges Riksbank, with its eKrona project, appears to have gone furthest in thinking about the potential issuance of a retail CBCC.

A retail CBCC along the lines of Fedcoin would eliminate the high price volatility that is common to cryptocurrencies. Moreover, as Koning (2014) notes, Fedcoin has the potential to relieve the zero lower bound constraint on monetary policy. As with other electronic forms of central bank money, it is technically possible to pay interest on a DLT-based CBCC. If a retail CBCC were to completely replace cash, it would no longer be possible for depositors to avoid negative interest rates and still hold central bank money.[183]

We will discuss the campaign to go cashless in the next section, but note above that if physical cash is replaced with a CBCC, it would be possible for the bank to charge a negative interest rate for the "right" to own the CBCC.

Whatever the fate of Bitcoin and the other altcoins, the central banks of the world have clearly indicated their interest in using this technology for their own purposes. Starting at the top with the Bank for International Settlements, they all recognize the possibilities inherent with a CBCC. The only substantive question that remains is who will operate the digital warehouse where the trillions of blockchain transactions will be stored.

The BIS noted the disruptive potential for commercial banks that are unable to compete with larger bank strategies. This

---

183 *BIS Quarterly Review*, "Central bank cryptocurrencies", Bech and Garratt, September 17, 2017,.

would lead to a massive consolidation of banks everywhere, driving smaller banks to be taken over or simply put out of business. The 2008 financial crisis exposed the predatory nature of the largest global banks when many smaller banks were crushed. Eliminating competition is thus another carrot for adoption of CBCC.

The United Nations opines about the trillions of dollars of non-monetized assets in the world, such as forests and other natural resources. While Bitcoins are created out of thin air by solving complex mathematical equations, blockchain can be used to create value based on anything that is verifiable. This is called "asset tokenization" and is growing in popularity around the world.

Basically, anything can be tokenized and turned into blockchain currency. One blogger shares this example:

Tokenization on Blockchain is a steady trend of 2018. It seems that everything is being tokenized on Blockchain from paintings, diamonds and company stocks to real estate.

Imagine that you have some property—say an apartment. You need cash quickly. The apartment is valued at $150,000 but you just need $10,000.

Enter tokenization. Tokenization is a method that converts rights to an asset into a digital token. Suppose there is a $200,000 apartment. Tokenization can transform this apartment into 200,000 tokens (the number is totally arbitrary, we could have issued 2 million tokens). Thus, each token represents a 0.0005% share of the underlying asset. Finally, we issue the token on some sort of a platform supporting smart contracts, for example on Ethereum, so that the tokens can be freely bought and sold on different exchanges. When you buy one token, you actually buy 0.0005% of the ownership in the asset. Buy 100,000 tokens and you own 50% of the assets. Buy all 200,000 tokens and you are 100% owner of the asset. Obviously, you are not becoming a legal owner of the property. However, because Blockchain is a public ledger that is immutable, it ensures that once you buy tokens, nobody can "erase" your ownership even if it is not registered in a gov-

ernment-run registry. It should be clear now why Blockchain enables this type of services.[184]

There are a myriad of startup companies already specializing in tokenizing such diverse assets as real estate, alternative energy, commodities, art, intellectual property, and even people. In these cases, the locked-up value in these assets is suddenly released through tokenization, even though the original owners still control the asset. That these schemes are fraught with complications of ownership and property rights is immaterial: people are buying it!

Carbon credit systems have failed miserably in the past 10 years. One company, Veridium, is changing that by using blockchain technology to tokenize carbon credits, which could possibly be a precursor to an energy-based currency. One journal describes how this could drive Sustainable Development:

A carbon credit is a license for a country or organization to emit a particular volume of greenhouse gases. In the same way that blockchain allows the tokenization of other real-life assets such as real estate or diamonds, Veridium creates tokens that represent carbon credits, allowing easy international trading.

The company will also calculate the exact value of carbon credit that a company needs to offset its carbon footprint. From a corporate perspective, this reduces the barrier to using carbon credits and allows a quantitative measure of achieving sustainability objectives.[185]

The United Nations and their member nations will soon discover tokenization as they realize that they can pledge vast swaths of natural resources to be tokenized. This could create hundreds of trillions of dollars in liquid assets that could finance all of Sustainable Development and then some. For instance, the rainforest in Brazil covers approximately 11.8 billion acres. At $2,000 per acre, this alone could be monetized for $23.6 trillion. The US government owns 640 million acres of land, represent-

184 *Coinmonks*, "Asset Tokenization on Blockchain Explained in Plain English, May 19, 2018.
185 *NextBigFuture*, "The Blockchain Race Towards a More Sustainable World", Brian Wang, October 16, 2018.

ing about 28% of our land mass and untold wealth in resources. Could the Federal Reserve collude with the U.S. Government to tokenize its land ownership? Absolutely.

Converting Natural Capital

On June 28, 2014 California Governor Jerry Brown signed AB-129 into law. Called the Alternative Currencies Act, it repealed existing law that "prohibited anyone from issuing or putting in circulation, as money, anything but the lawful money of the United States."[186] With this, California became the first state to specifically allow the creation of alternative currencies.

The Sustainable Economies Law Center had lobbied for AB-129 for two years, stating that "our centralized monetary system is fundamentally flawed. 97% of our money supply is put into circulation as debt by private for-profit banks, who control where that money first enters our economy."[187]

In 2015, another non-profit organization sprang up in California called The EarthDollar Alliance, which intends to soon launch the Earth Dollar as an asset-backed global cryptocurrency. According to its website,

Earth Dollar ("ED") is different than most fiat currencies because it is backed by Natural Capital Assets within our World Heritage Sanctuaries. The Earth Dollar's value is secured against "Natural Capital Assets", which will be placed in a global commons, held in a trust, and safeguarded indefinitely for the benefit of Planet Earth and all the life it supports. Global Commons is a term typically used to describe international, supranational, and global resource domains in which common-pool resources are found. Global commons include the earth's shared natural resources, such as the high oceans, the atmosphere, and outer space. Cyberspace may also meet the definition of a global commons.[188]

186 California Legislative Information, AB-129 Lawful Money, (2013-2014).
187 Sustainable Economies Law Center website, "The California Alternative Currencies Act.
188 EarthDollar.org website, "Living Economic System".

Although ED claims that it is "asset-backed", no holder of the currency will ever see any of those assets. The ED website pledges total support for the United Nations Sustainable Development Goals, the World Bank's Natural Capital Accounting System and World Basic Income, which is similar to Universal Basic Income but global in application. EarthDollar's mission statement is very clear:

> We are ushering a new alternative Living Economic System centered on the wellbeing of all life on our planet... The Earth Dollar is asset-backed, self-regulating, decentralized, open and takes action on climate change. It creates intrinsic value by rewarding restoration and preservation of the Earth in order to overcome poverty and to create a sustainable world. [189]

Furthermore, ED claims that it has coded the following laws directly into its blockchain:

- Universal Declaration of Rights of Mother Earth
- Universal Declaration of Human Rights
- Universal Declaration of Rights of Indigenous Peoples
- Constitution of Mother Earth

Since the EarthDollar has not officially launched yet, it remains to be seen just how successful it will be. Their plans are ambitious with over €3 trillion of so-called Natural Capital pledged to the initial valuation. However, even if EarthDollar is a big dud, it has said all the right things about financing the UN's Sustainable Development Goals; certainly others will follow in its path.

Other Examples

The city of Berkeley is funding its Affordable Housing[190] program by issuing a cryptocurrency against its municipal bonds. If successful, the city will be the pioneer of a new wave of public financing. The cryptocurrency would be government issued and

---

189 Ibid.
190 Compare Affordable Housing to UN Sustainable Development Goal #11, Make cities and human settlements inclusive, safe, resilient and sustainable.

publicly tradable. Hundreds of other U.S. cities are at the ready to jump in with their own programs. One journalist writes:

> *Cities face a milieu of technical, bureaucratic and financial hurdles that can stall public infrastructure, lead to public catastrophes and support increased inequality. Blockchain can fundamentally revolutionize how local governments restructure institutions and asset flows, creating cities that are safer, more equitable and more globally competitive.*[191]

Cryptocurrency is rapidly working its way into Public-Private Partnerships as a means of financing and paying subcontractors. The state and city of São Paulo are using a token called Buildcoin to pay contractors in Brazil as well as around the world. According to one report,

> *A former informal advisor to U.S. President Donald Trump on infrastructure issues, Norm Anderson argues that the buildcoin model, if successful, could be deployed outside of Brazil to help solve the massive worldwide problem of infrastructure underinvestment.*
>
> *Global infrastructure investment falls short of target by an estimated $1 trillion a year, and in the U.S., the American Society of Civil Engineers reckons that $3.6 trillion in spending is needed over the next five years just to maintain and upgrade existing infrastructure.*[192]

The potential of this new technology is so great that universities, think-tanks, banks and even entire nations (i.e., United Arab Emirates) are jumping in with abandon. The wisdom or foolishness of this is immaterial for this discussion, but we must recognize it for what it is: **Cryptocurrency is the futuristic financing tool of Sustainable Development.**

---

191 Medium, "How blockchain and automation can deliver better, safer public/private partnerships", Aaron Lewis, April 16, 2018.

192 Coindesk, "Why São Paulo Wants to Pay for Infrastructure with Cryptocurrency", January 19, 2018.

Cashless Society

Historically, physical cash has provided a lot of security and comfort to its holders. There is no trace of activity when you spend it; it reduces your risk of loss due to bank failure or scandal; it is universally acceptable. Furthermore, it is the *only* financial instrument for those who are not part of the banking system in the first place. It is estimated that 2 billion adults, or 35 percent of the total, are "unbanked" around the world. This represents a huge and untouched market for digital bankers, but until now, there has been no sure way to force the unbanked to give up their independence by eliminating cash altogether, until now.

As the BIS alluded to above, a CBBC has the ability to completely replace physical cash, but is it a specific goal of the global elite to do so? Indeed, it is. Every continent on earth is in one stage or another in removing cash altogether. In China, as much as 95% of all consumer transactions are cashless. In India, all large denomination bills have been removed from circulation, as is also the case in the United States where the $100 bill is the largest denomination. "No cash accepted" signs have popped up all over Europe, while Finland, Denmark and Sweden expect to be completely cashless in a few years. Airlines have gone cashless for inflight purchases. Many restaurants in America now have cashless signs in the window, forcing consumers to pay electronically.

The leading Fintech journal in Australia indicates, "Australia to be a cashless society by 2022". The main reason for this is consumers voluntary application of Fintech:

> *Two years later and consumers now have a plethora of convenient payment options available including PayPass and tap and go technology, digital wallets such as Apple Pay, Samsung Pay and Android Pay and wearable technologies such as the Apple Watch, the Inamo Curl and even Visa's WaveShades.*
>
> ***This decline in cash payments is largely fueled by the introduction of these new payment technologies,*** *says head of market analysis at East & Partners Martin Smith.*

*"As consumers continue to embrace platforms such as wearables, contactless payments and mobile payments, and they're further integrated into everyday life, **the need to carry cash will continue to diminish at an accelerated rate,**" said Smith.*[193] [emphasis added]

In 2017, Visa launched the *Visa Cashless Challenge* targeting restaurants in America where 50 winners were given $10,000 each for envisioning ways to cease taking cash in favor of electronic payment only. With the contest ended and prizes paid, Visa announced on its website,

*Representing every corner of the country, from the plains of Ohio, to the bustling streets of Washington D.C., to the seven hills of San Francisco, the winners of Visa's Cashless Challenge have one thing in common: **they share Visa's vision and see the promise of a cash-free future.***[194] [emphasis added]

Thus, we can see that the disappearance of cash is a push-pull phenomenon: governments removing large bills making it difficult for hoarding wealth and secondly, the growth of mesmerizing technology that offers compelling convenience in place of cash. Fintech is driving both ends against the middle.

But, why? Looking past the lure of convenience, efficiency and safety, we find Technocrats poised like children waiting to get into the candy store. *The Atlantic* described what's inside that store:

*In a cashless society, the cash has been converted into numbers, into signals, into electronic currents. In short: **Information replaces cash.***

Information is lightning-quick. It crosses cities, states, and national borders in the twinkle of an eye. It passes through many kinds of devices, flowing from phone to phone, and computer to computer, rather than being sealed away in those silent marble temples we used to call banks. Information never jangles uncomfortably in your pocket.

---

193 *Australian FinTech*, "Australia to be a cashless society by 2020", Allison Banney, April 26, 2017.
194 Visa Cashless Challenge, https://usa.visa.com/about-visa/cashless.html

*But wherever information gathers and flows, two predators follow closely behind it: censorship and surveillance. The case of digital money is no exception. **Where money becomes a series of signals, it can be censored; where money becomes information, it will inform on you.**[195]* [emphasis added]

With all of this in mind, it is worthwhile to review three of the seven original requirements of Technocracy declared in 1934:

- *Provide a specific registration of the type, kind, etc., of all goods and services, where produced, and where used.*
- *Provide specific registration of the consumption of each individual, plus a record and description of the individual.*
- *Distribute goods and services to every member of the population.*[196]

The first two items call for very detailed surveillance and tracking of everything produced and consumed. The last item uses the familiar "every member", meaning that there must be no one left out of the system. The UN stresses inclusiveness as a major doctrine of Sustainable Development: UNICEF and UNESCO call for "No child left behind"; the Sustainable Development goals promise "access to energy for all", "nutritious food for all", "wellbeing for all", "decent work for all", "opportunities for all", "better quality of life for all" and "water and sanitation for all". [197]

Fintech and Islam

Not surprisingly, the most unbanked populations in the world are found in the Mideast, in large part because traditional western banking is not compatible with Sharia law. Here are some examples with unbanked percentages noted: Egypt (85%), Pakistan (87%), Cameroon (88%), Afghanistan (90%), Burundi (93%), Yemen (93%) and Turkmenistan (98.2%).[198]

---

195 *The Atlantic*, "How a Cashless Society Could Embolden Big Brother", Sarah Heong, April 8, 2016.
196 *Technocracy Study Course*, Technocracy, Inc., 1934, p. 225-226.
197 United Nations, Sustainable Development Goals website
198 World Economic Forum, "The world's unbanked, in 6 charts", September 6, 2017.

The principles of Fintech are peculiarly adaptable to Sharia finance, leading to a surge in Fintech interest in the Islamic world. Sharia finance does not permit charging interest, for instance, but does allow for trading, fee-based transactions and leasing. Since Fintech is highly oriented toward transactions and fees, it is fertile ground for Islamic promotion.

Leaders in Islamic Fintech include Bahrain, Abu Dhabi, Dubai, Malaysia, and Saudi Arabia. This led *Forbes* to conclude in late 2017 that *Fintech Is The New Oil In The Middle East And North Africa,* and specifically ties Islamic Fintech to reaching the unbanked:

> ...despite the ubiquity of smartphones and internet connectivity, 86% of the adult population in the region is unbanked, while three in four GCC bank customers are ready to switch banks for a better digital experience.
>
> Boosting financial inclusion is crucial for economic diversity and growth across the region. Moussa Beidas, co-founder of Dubai-based startup Bridg, which allows smartphone-to-smartphone payments using bluetooth, says fintech has become an innovative way to bridge the divide and provide cheaper services to the unbanked.[199]

Green Economy

There are many definitions of green economy but they all point back to Sustainable Development. The UN states that it "improves human well-being and social inclusion, while significantly reducing environmental risks and ecological scarcities."[200]

The UN Environmental Programme (UNEP) elaborates further:

> An Inclusive Green Economy is an alternative to today's dominant economic model, which generates widespread environmental and health risks, encourages wasteful consumption and production, drives ecological and resource scarci-

---

199 *Forbes*, "Fintech Is The New Oil In The Middle East And North Africa", Suprana D'Chunha, December 11, 2017.
200 United Nations Economic Commission for Europe, Green Economy website.

*ties and results in inequality. It is an opportunity to advance both sustainability and social equity as functions of a **stable and prosperous financial system** within the contours of a finite and fragile planet. It is a pathway towards achieving the 2030 Agenda for Sustainable Development, eradicating poverty while safeguarding the ecological thresholds, which underpin human health, well-being, and development.*[201] [emphasis added]

The "stable and prosperous financial system" that underpins and finances Sustainable Development is Fintech and it is being embraced by every major segment of society on Earth.

---

201 United Nations Environmental Programme, "What is an 'Inclusive Green Economy?'", website.

CHAPTER 9

LIVING IN A FISHBOWL

Suspicionless surveillance does not become okay simply because it's only victimizing 95% of the world instead of 100%. - Edward Snowden

Dave woke up at 6:00AM and speaks to his personal digital assistant, "Alexa, play some Ed Sheeran music." Alexa complies within seconds, and the first soundtrack begins to play. As he turned on the shower, the water heater immediately started drawing electricity through the new Smart Meter on the side of his house. The AI program at Dave's utility company, Acme Electric, recognizes the device 'signature' and model and was able to immediately compare his unit to those of his local and extended neighbors.

As Dave turned on his computer to check his Gmail account, his router address went live and alerted his ISP and the cable company. "Good morning, Dave, all is well with Internet connectivity this morning." After reading and replying to a few important emails from co-workers and customers, Gmail faithfully deposited his activity on Google's cloud servers while simultaneously scanning each email for certain content or trigger words. As he checks a couple of web sites, Dave casually notices a popup ad for a high-efficiency water heater. He thinks, "I ought to check out replacing my old water heater someday", but he is too late to to anything about it right now.

After jumping into his car at 7:30 AM, he grabs his smartphone and uses Google Maps to plot the best-route to his first customer. When he arrives, Google records his time of arrival and the exact route he actually took to get there; he didn't notice that he had passed 2 hidden license plate readers that captured his plate number, including one at the toll booth to get on the freeway. On the way, he made a quick phone call to schedule a new prospect on the other side of town; Google notes the new connection.

Dave's first meeting goes well, but he is given a big project to organize for which he takes prolific meeting notes in his Google Docs account. He figures he will sort it all out when he gets back at the office, but he assures himself that he will have enough detail to get started.

 After fitting in one more customer call, Dave arrives at his office and takes a restful break in order to eat lunch and kick back with his laptop computer. As he opens his personal Gmail account, he notices an ad for a high-efficiency water heater.

"That's strange", he thinks. "This is the second thing I've seen today about water heaters."

Next, he spots an official looking email from the Department of Transportation which he opens immediately: it informs him that he is being fined for not paying the toll when he got on the freeway at 7:50 AM, and includes a clear picture of his face in the driver's seat. It tersely reports, "We have matched your license plate to your account, and verified that you were, in fact, the driver of this vehicle". As he curses under his breath, he takes off for his afternoon customer visits.

On the way, he makes a few extra stops. He gets gas at a mini-mart, buys some snacks and then makes a quick stop at Walmart to pick up some drain cleaner to fix the sink in the guest bathroom. Since he used his debit card, the detail of every purchase is duly recorded by his bank. And so the afternoon goes until Dave heads home tired but feeling pretty good about the day's activities, even if a little aggravated about his picture being taken at that toll booth.

Checking his personal Gmail account as he turns on the TV, he immediately sees three more ads for high-efficiency water heaters and immediately thinks "What the heck is up with this? Why am I being bombarded for ads about water heaters?" The next email that pops in that offers the first clue:

Dear Dave,

Your American Water heater, model G61050T40, is 20 years old and 5 years beyond its specified life-cycle. According to our energy efficiency policies we must increase your bill by 10% to adjust for the extra energy consumption.

However, we would be happy to assist you in choosing a new and efficient model that meets all Energy Star specifications. If you install a new water heater, we will be happy to waive the 10% surcharge and give you an extra 10% credit on your next bill.

Thank you for being our customer.

Kind regards,

Acme Utility Company

As he scratches his head, he remembers that Acme replaced his analog electric meter with a new digital "Smart Meter" just last week.

"I've owned this house for 10 years and *nobody* knows what kind of water heater I have or don't have", he thinks, "The only way Acme could find this out is from that stupid Smart Meter!"

"Dang, and those rats sold my information to those marketing companies to hustle me for new water heaters."

Dave is having a bad day, but it isn't over yet. His phone rings and it's a local number so he answers.

"Hi Dave, this is Bill from ABC Plumbing and we are specialists in clearing all kinds of clogged plumbing issues". He says, "we are going to be in your area in the morning, and if you have any plumbing problems, we would be happy to stop by and give you a hand."

"Oh, and by the way, we are also running a great special on high-efficiency water heaters this week!"

Dave slammed the phone down as he took a deep breath, heart pounding.

"Walmart and my bank are selling my data too?"

After dinner, Dave decides to do a little recreational browsing and pulls up Google Chrome on his laptop. He clicks the bookmark for his favorite news site and up pops an add for project management software.

"Hey, this is the same software that my first appointment wants me to use for their new project. But, I didn't tell anybody about..."

Mid-thought it occurs to him that the only place he mentioned the project *or* the name of the software was in his meeting notes on Google Docs, to which nobody has access but him.

"What's happening to my life", he yelled, "why do I feel like I am living in a fishbowl?"

"Dave, this is Alexa", says a soothing voice from the living room, "I can tell that you are upset. Would it help to hear some more music from Ed Sheeran?"

The Fourth Amendment of the U.S. Constitution offers very specific protection to citizens on the sanctity of their persons and domicile. It states,

> *The right of the people to be secure in their persons, houses, papers, and effects, against unreasonable searches and seizures, shall not be violated, and no Warrants shall issue, but upon probable cause, supported by Oath or affirmation, and particularly describing the place to be searched, and the persons or things to be seized.*

Unfortunately, Technocrats hate and routinely ignore the Constitution. If they were to conduct themselves within the confines of the Fourth Amendment, there would be no ubiquitous and secret surveillance anywhere, no harvesting and aggregating your life's data and thus, there would be no data with which to socially engineer your entire life.

Most people have no concept of what is happening around them nor how it intends to control them. They are largely in a state of bewilderment, exhibiting symptoms similar to what psychologists call "retreat from reality" where relations with the real world are substituted with imaginary satisfactions or fantasy.

In 1970, futurists Alvin and Heidi Toffler wrote a best-selling book called *Future Shock*. It has since sold over 6 million copies and has been translated into several foreign languages. They defined a psychological state of individuals and societies when they experienced "too much change in to short a period of time."[202] In other words, excessively rapid change induces a state of shock that interferes with normal mental and emotional processes such as "shattering stress and disorientation." Toffler extrapolated that "The illiterate of the future will not be the person who cannot read. It will be the person who does not know how to learn". Indeed, the concept of future shock is upon us, and Toffler nailed it: "The great growling engine of change - technology."

Advancing technology has made ubiquitous surveillance possible, but few expected it to expand in such a short period of time. There are several interrelated inventions that have made it possible. First is the technology used to examine the social environment: advanced surveillance cameras and facial recognition software. Second is artificial intelligence (AI) software: self-learning and deep-learning algorithms can make sense of just about anything that lives or moves. Third is the technology of advanced computer processing: AI computer chips, massive data storage and massively parallel supercomputers.

While all of these technologies might have beneficial uses for mankind, in the hands of Technocrats they offer a unique opportunity for total social control and domination. While this is already happening in the U.S, it is most obvious in the Technocracy nation of China.

---

202 NBC News, "Future Shock Author Alvin Toffler Dies at 87", Alex Johnson, June 29, 2016.

In December 2017, China had installed 176 million surveillance cameras nationwide. By July 2018, there were 200 million installed. The trajectory is to have 626 million installed by 2020. Considering that there are 1.38 billion people in China, there will be one surveillance camera for every 2.2 people and more than one camera for every family. Does this seem like overkill? China's entire surveillance network is connected to a series of specially-designed facial recognition computers equipped with advanced AI software that can identify and locate any citizen within minutes of issuing the command. As I wrote in Technocracy News and Trends,

A challenge experiment was just conducted in Guiyang, China to see how long it would take to locate and capture a BBC reporter who was mixed in at random with the general population of 3.5 million people. After the police snapped his picture and fed it into the massive facial recognition database, which contains the facial image of every Guiyang resident, the reporter took off. They gave him a head start as he mingled in on the crowded city streets; then a request for his apprehension was given to the computer equipped with the latest AI security software.

The AI software combed through millions of images from tens of thousands of cameras in Guiyang, all transmitted back to the master computer, hunting for the reporter. The results were shocking.

It took a total of 7 minutes before police physically apprehended him. Assuming it took a few minutes for police to assemble and walk/run to his location, the actual identification could have taken as little as two minutes. Yes, just two minutes to find a single subject in a city of 3.5 million!

Yin Jun, executive with surveillance camera manufacturer Dahua Technology, stated,

"We can match every face with an ID card and trace all your movements back one week in time. We can match your face with your car, match you with your relatives and the people

you're in touch with. With enough cameras, we can know who you frequently meet."

The next Orwellian layer to appear on top of the physical surveillance network is a system of Social Credit Scoring (SCS) that some have called the "gamification of trust". SCS requires massive data collection on every citizen in China, including all financial transaction, events attended, social interactions, friendships and data-mining of social media activities. Much of this data is collected in conjunction with the surveillance network, i.e., be careful who you meet in public.

As massive AI computers analyze all this ever-changing and ever-growing mountain of "big data", a Social Credit Score is calculated and assigned to each citizen. The score can go up or down whenever a different calculation is received. Some things that might affect a citizen's score include:

- Do you pay your debts on time?
- Are your personal finances in line with your occupation?
- Have you received tickets for things like jaywalking?
- Have you criticized or praised the government?
- Are you a Christian, Muslim or atheist?
- Do you hang out with others who have a low SCS?
- Are you community-oriented or individualistic?
- Do you do things out of your ordinary observed behavior?

If you are a model citizen in China, your score might approach the maximum level of 700. If the computer decides that you are a troublemaker, you might be lucky to receive a score of 200. High SCS holders will have travel freedoms, will attend better schools and get better jobs. Low SCS holders will not be allowed to have travel passes, live in better housing, get into better schools and will be left with less desirable work conditions.

This system has already been switched on in China and will approach 100 percent efficiency and penetration of the population by 2020. This means that every individual can be forced to comply with government expectations, or else.

This is Scientific Dictatorship, pure and simple.

Like Americans, most Chinese citizens are also suffering from Future Shock. According to a Chinese investigative journalist,

> You can see from the Chinese people's mental state. Their eyes are blinded and their ears are blocked. They know little about the world and live in an illusion.[203]

When interviewed about Social Credit Scoring, one Shanghai-based saleswoman told NPR that "As long as it doesn't violate my privacy, I'm okay with it."[204] Obviously, she is living in an illusion and doesn't even know it.

Future Shock notwithstanding, China portends serious problems for America because it is exporting its technology en-mass back to the U.S. Not surprisingly, much of their technological know-how was either invented in the U.S. in the first place or stolen from it. Ten years ago, virtually all such surveillance schemes were illegal in the U.S., but now most of those barriers have been broken down. The common bond between Technocrats in both countries guarantees a smooth reintroduction into American society.

In 2016, China began to run pre-crime algorithms on its massive collection of social data in order to find out who would be most likely to commit a crime. One journalist describes it like this:

> The Chinese government wants to know about everything: every text a person sends, every extra stop they make on the way home. It's designed for dissidents, but it means that they'll know every time a smoker buys a pack of cigarettes, how much gas a car owner uses, what time the new mom goes to bed, and what's in the bachelor's refrigerator.
>
> It's a scary thought, especially when you consider that the main target of Chinese pre-crime efforts wouldn't be "terror-

---

203 Science Alert, "China's Chilling 'Social Credit System' Is Straight Out of Dystopian Sci-Fi, And It's Already Switched On", Peter Dockrill, September 20, 2018.
204 Ibid.

ists," *murderers, rapists, or child molesters, but rather dissidents of every shape and size.*[205]

On the other hand, *Forbes* reveals the current state of pre-crime analysis in modern America:

> *Data, not psychic energy, drives today's pre-crime technology. Law professor Andrew Guthrie Ferguson describes predictive policing "as an attempt to apply a public health approach to violence. Just as epidemiological patterns reveal environmental toxins that can increase health risks (like getting cancer), criminal patterns can increase life risks (like getting shot)."*

> *Predictive policing requires sifting through data to identify both key risk factors and the conditions under which crimes are likely to result. Law enforcement already uses statistics to determine which roads and neighborhoods to patrol more frequently, but modern predictive policing takes this to a whole new level of scope and precision.*[206]

Dozens of cities across America have already implemented pre-crime software to catch offenders before they offend, including Los Angeles, San Francisco, Chicago, New York City, New Orleans, Atlanta and a host of smaller cities. It's here, it's now and it's spreading like wildfire.

Another lookalike technology is mobile robocop units that are equipped with a plethora of sensors including multiple cameras, AI and facial recognition cameras. A company started in Silicon Valley in 2013, Knightscope, develops autonomous security robots "to predict and prevent crime utilizing autonomous robots, analytics and engagement."[207] Their robotic units are called a 'force multiplier" by "providing an autonomous physical presence, gathering data from the environment in real-time, and pushing anomalies to our user interface, the Knightscope Security Operations Center."[208] By 2018, Knightscope's robocop units have

205 *Daily Beast*, "China Wants to Make 'Minority Report' a Reality", G. Clay Whitaker, March 13, 2016.
206 *Forbes*, "The Future Of Policing Using Pre-Crime Technology", Kenneth Coats, August 14, 2018.
207 Knightscope.com website, "Our Story".
208 Ibid.

been sold in 16 states in America and several megacities like New York and Los Angeles.

Not to be outdone, China debuted their first robocop model in early 2017 that was developed by the National Defense University. The "AnBot" looks suspiciously like Knightscope's robots but they will be rapidly rolled out nationwide to augment the stationary camera network.

Robocops are beyond the novelty phase in the Mideast. Dubai has been testing sophisticated police robots built by Pal Robotics in Barcelona. If current testing is successful, Dubai claims that robocops will make up 25 percent of its patrolling force by 2030. The same theme features instant facial recognition, several types of cameras and sensors.

The problem with computer modeling of any kind, including pre-crime predictions, is that it is not even close to being 100 percent accurate. This means it makes mistakes that can directly harm the lives of innocent people. This shortfall is well known within the technology world, but the Technocrat mind figures that 80 percent accuracy is better than letting more crimes being committed. There is no ethical consideration for the falsely accused or overly surveilled citizens. However, this is absolutely unconstitutional and in some cases, illegal as well. The Fourteenth Amendment guarantees "equal protection under the law". The Fifth Amendment guarantees "due process under the law." The Fourth Amendment, as noted above, prohibits "unreasonable searches and seizures."

Hoovering up and analyzing all citizen data without cause or warrant in order to predict offenders would cause the Founding Fathers of America to roll over in their graves. Unfortunately, Technocrats have no respect or regard for the U.S. Constitution or the Founding Fathers. The unalienable rights mentioned in the Declaration of Independence are anathema to Technocrats because it elevates human sanctity and dignity above all else.

Smart Cities Are Special

Smart cities raise a series of problems. First of all, the right to privacy is entirely redefined in a smart city, as they create an environment where we are no longer expected to consent to the collecting, processing, and sharing of our data but instead the minute we step in the streets we are exposed to both government and corporate surveillance. And not only is there no opting out but more likely than not you will not even know that data about you is being collected.[209]

Smart Cities are being inundated with technology way beyond just biometric camera systems. Driven by Big Tech, cities are adopting sensor technology that will measure every aspect of city life. Sensors are being built into light poles, street corners, bus and train stops, public service vehicles and neighborhoods. Smart Grid technology monitors all usage of electricity, natural gas and water. Smart buildings are being retrofitted with sensors that monitor everything that happens on every floor, from person movement to elevators to air conditioning. Collectively, this adequately showcases the so-called "Internet of Things" (IoT) that will come to life as 5G wireless technology is rolled out. In fact, the IoT *is* Smart City technology!

The Chief Technology Officer of Teradata, a major data analytics provider, stated,

The bottom line is that sensor technology in the IoT context is key. When I say IoT context I mean that we get a view of the whole city across these different domains of the life of the city as it's captured in the sensor data.[210]

The IoT, sometimes called the Internet of Everything, literally connects everything into a single database with multiple viewing angles. To all of the things mentioned above, add smart phones, laptop computers, routers, credit or debit card readers, store transactions, items tagged with RFID chips, and so on.

---

209 Privacy International, U.K., "Case Study: Smart Cities and Our Brave New World", 2018.
210 *Information Age*, "Smart City Technology: It's all about the Internet of Things", Nick Ismail, August 14, 2018.

Most Smart City 'designers' have worried about the one thing that could block their implementation efforts: lack of connectivity. This risk is completely nullified with the new 5G wireless communication standard that will be fully rolled out to America by the end of 2019. 5G is far more than just a smart phone carrier. It will allow any physical device to be data-integrated at speeds approaching that of fiber optic. 5G is 23 times faster than 4G technology, approaching 50 gigabytes per second. However, the real breakthrough in 5G has to do with "latency", or the turnaround time to initiate a transfer. With 4G, typical latency is 50 milliseconds. 5G turns the same packet around in 1 millisecond! This is an improvement of 50 times.

When the IoT is fully enabled with 5G technology, the entire data feed, no matter how large, will be instantaneous. Thus, today's AI supercomputers will be able to model the entire city's activities in real time.

Geospatial intelligence (GEOINT)

The drive to Smart City transformation entails all of the above mentioned technology into a relatively new discipline called Geospatial Intelligence (GEOINT), and it is being used extensively in attempting to manage the hoards of people in urban environments. GEOINT was originally conceived as a discipline by the U.S. military for military purposes of "Mastering The Human Domain" on the battlefield. The term was coined in 2011 by former Director of National Intelligence, Lt. Gen. James Clapper (USAF, Ret.). At the time, he was the head of the National Geospatial-Intelligence Agency in Springfield, Virginia. Here is the department's original and official definition:

GEOINT encompasses all aspects of imagery (including capabilities formerly referred to as Advanced Geospatial Intelligence and imagery-derived MASINT) and geospatial information and services (GI&S); formerly referred to as mapping, charting, and geodesy). It includes, but is not limited to, data ranging from the ultraviolet through the mi-

crowave portions of the electromagnetic spectrum, as well as information derived from the analysis of literal imagery; geospatial data; georeferenced social media; and information technically derived from the processing, exploitation, literal, and non-literal analysis of spectral, spatial, temporal, radiometric, phase history, polarimetric data, fused products (products created out of two or more data sources), and the ancillary data needed for data processing and exploitation, and signature information (to include development, validation, simulation, data archival, and dissemination). These types of data can be collected on stationary and moving targets by electro-optical (to include IR, MWIR, SWIR TIR, Spectral, MSI, HSI, HD), SAR (to include MTI), related sensor programs (both active and passive) and non-technical means (to include geospatial information acquired by personnel in the field).[211]

GEOINT is closely related to traditional concepts of geography where all immoveable features and objects in the landscape are mapped. Such fixed mapping allows us to reliably get from point A to point B on a consistent basis. Neither point A or B are expected to change locations. In a much broader context, GEOINT attempts to factor in all moveable objects, including cars, trucks and airplanes but most importantly, humans. Humans are never in the same place for very long, especially in modern society.

GEOINT literally maps the entire human domain and overlays it onto traditional mapping systems. By tracking the location of all people in the targeted system, they quickly subdivide into naturally associated groups and networks. These could represent any group such as friend or family networks, social groups, religious affiliations, political meetings, etc. When you observe people long enough with enough detail, not only do their personal patterns emerge, but also their relationships to the groups to which they belong are soon observed to follow their own patterns.

---

211 Memorandum for Principal Director of National Intelligence, Deputy Director of National Intelligence for Collection, from James R. Clapper, Lieutenant General, USAF (Ret.), Director [NGA] 17 October 2005, gwg.nga.mil.

What GEOINT attempts to do is locate the behavioral anomalies that would warrant closer analysis. The problem is that it demands knowledge of all normal behavior patterns and thus, total surveillance of all people. On the battlefield, for instance, imagine our military carefully watching a suspected enemy cell that might launch an attack. As long as normal patterns are observed, there is no alarm, but when a few of the members stray outside those patterns, it would indicate something unusual is happening. If those outliers were seen amassing ammunition, for instance, it would set off alarm bells.

Another key element of GEOINT is satellite and drone imagery. While these may not identify each individual, they can still note broader changes taking place in the overall landscape. Coupled with on-the-ground intelligence, imagery can take on significant meaning.

Thanks to data-hungry Technocrat social engineers, civilian populations all over the world are now coming under the microscope of geospatial tracking and analysis, or GEOINT. The Smart City initiatives in America would be instantly regurgitated by cities if citizens understood that "Mastering the Human Domain" has them playing the part of the human domain to be mastered.

Notably, the field of GEOINT has grown so fast that 17 universities now have degree or certificate programs available, including Penn State, University of North Carolina, University of Maryland, University of Utah, University of Southern California, John Hopkins, George Mason University, University of Texas and University of Missouri. Many of these programs are a subsidiary of geography departments but with a crossover to Information Technologies.

One prominent GEOINT pioneer is Dr. Jerome E. Dobson, emeritus professor of geography at the University of Kansas, former Distinguished Research Fellow at the Oak Ridge National Laboratory and President of the American Geographical Society. Since the field of GEOINT was identified in 2011, Dobson has been considered a pioneer.

However, even before GEOINT was a defined discipline, Dobson wrestled with the ethical issues of his own field of Geographic Information Systems (GIS). In 2003, eight years before Gen. Clapper's declaration of GEOINT, Dobson wrote a paper with colleague Peter F. Fisher titled "Geoslavery". They wrote;

Human tracking devices, however, introduce a new potential for real-time control that extends far beyond privacy and surveillance, per se. As a result, society must contemplate a new form of slavery characterized by location control. Geoslavery now looms as a real, immediate, and global threat.[212]

Society has failed to contemplate geoslavery, even though it has had ample opportunity and reason to do so. Concluding that geoslavery is the "ultimate fulfillment of George Orwell's Big Brother nightmare", they note that, instead of watching 20 or 30 people at a time, Location Based Services (LBS) can monitor thousands or even millions simultaneously. Today, as in China, we could raise the count into the billions.

In the Smart City of tomorrow, people will indeed be living in a fishbowl: tracked, monitored, analyzed, nudged, limited and directed. They will be told what to think, how to think, when to think and how they are allowed to speak. Non-conformists will be conformed or shunned. Trouble-makers will simply be excluded altogether.

---

212 *IEEE Technology and Society Magazine*, "Geoslavery", Dobson and Fisher, Spring 2003, pp. 47-52.

Chapter 10

Worshipping the Creation

And they served their idols: which were
a snare unto them. (Psalms 108:36)

No discussion of Technocracy, Sustainable Development or globalization would be complete without a discussion on spirituality. After all, history shows that man is a spiritual being with an innate urge to worship something greater than himself; those overlords who control societies and nations were fully aware of the power of religion to manipulate citizens.

The ancient Greek civilization, for instance, had a plethora of complex deities that became intricately interwoven into their entire culture. Although their various deities were quite different, everybody had a choice to follow one or more as his own personal god and then to attend all the functions, ceremonies and other activities at the local temples. In most Grecian cities, such idol temples were the main architectural attractions around which life was centered. Some familiar names to history buffs would include Zeus, Poseidon, Athena, Apollo, Artemis and Dionysus.

When Rome rose to power, many Greek gods were simply renamed and repurposed for Roman society: Zeus became Jupiter, Athena became Minerva, Poseidon became Neptune, Artemis became Diana, and so on.

Older civilizations in the Mideast and Asia are known to have worshiped idols with names like Dagon, Baal, Moloch, Ashtoreth and Marduk.

Despite the wild differences among these various systems of religion, there were obvious similarities. All were based on ideas and physical idols created by man himself. All ended up controlling their subjects to adhere to a particular political system. All had harsh physical penalties for heresy and non-compliance. All had some form of initiation or practice to demonstrate loyalty: The cult of Moloch, for instance, sacrificed their babies on the arms of its burning bronze altar; the cult of Aphrodite demonstrated worship by having sex with temple prostitutes.

When Technocrats in the 1930s bragged that they were so enlightened that they were non-religious, they totally misled their followers.[215] They had indeed abandoned the traditional forms of religion such as Christianity, but they did not somehow scientifically change their nature to have no need for worship.

The acknowledged father of Technocracy, Frenchman Henri de Saint-Simon (1760-1825), was also the forerunner of Scientism. You can see the first hints of this in a statement like:

A scientist, my dear friends, is a man who foresees; it is because science provides the means to predict that it is useful, and the scientists are superior to all other men.[216]

With the rise of Humanism in the early 1900s, Scientism was ready to burst forth in full array. Humanism basically said, "Look what man can do; who needs God?" Some scientists and engineers responded, "We can do plenty of things, just watch us." As the scientific revolution was producing new discoveries and inventions on an almost daily basis, public esteem for those scientists and engineers skyrocketed. At least a few of those truly believed that the only truth is scientific truth, or that which is revealed through science. However, is it really true that the Scientific Method alone can discover the truth, the whole truth and nothing but the truth?

---

215 For a thorough discussion, see Technocracy Rising: *The Trojan Horse of Global Transformation* by Patrick M. Wood

216 American Association for the Advancement of Science, "What is Scientism?", Thomas Burnett

The trouble started when some[217] scientists and engineers decided that their knowledge of the physical sciences somehow qualified them to become social engineers and design a new economic system such as Technocracy. This was a huge mistake, but it was the watershed for modern Scientism. One scholar wrote,

Central to scientism is the grabbing of nearly the entire territory of what were once considered questions that properly belong to philosophy. Scientism takes science to be not only better than philosophy at answering such questions, but the only means of answering them.[218]

Another elaborated further:

Science is an activity that seeks to explore the natural world using well-established, clearly-delineated methods. Given the complexity of the universe, from the very big to very small, from inorganic to organic, there is a vast array of scientific disciplines, each with its own specific techniques. The number of different specializations is constantly increasing, leading to more questions and areas of exploration than ever before. Science expands our understanding, rather than limiting it.

Scientism, on the other hand, is a speculative worldview about the ultimate reality of the universe and its meaning. Despite the fact that there are millions of species on our planet, scientism focuses an inordinate amount of its attention on human behavior and beliefs. Rather than working within carefully constructed boundaries and methodologies established by researchers, it broadly generalizes entire fields of academic expertise and dismisses many of them as inferior. With scientism, you will regularly hear explanations that rely on words like "merely", "only", "simply", or "nothing more than". Scientism restricts human inquiry.

Once you accept that science is the only source of human knowledge, you have adopted a philosophical position (scientism) that cannot be verified, or falsified, by science itself. It is, in a word, unscientific.[219]

217 Note: Not all scientists and engineers believe in Scientism and not all are Technocrats.
218 Austin L. Hughes, "The Folly of Scientism," *The New Atlantis*, Number 37, Fall 2012, pp. 32-50.
219 American Association for the Advancement of Science, "What is Scientism", Thomas Burnett, available at www.aaas.org.

For this very reason, Scientism is specifically hostile toward Christianity and pointedly rejects the Bible as truth. In China, where Technocracy has established deep roots, anti-Christian persecution is painfully evident. However, China *also* persecutes Muslims right along with the Christians because Islam also holds to a non-scientific worldview as well.

In sum, Technocracy subsumes Scientism as a religion where Technocrats represent the priesthood that worships the god of Science and Technology. While this seems to be a very rigid and narrow point of view, we will discover that it is merely the fountainhead of a multiplicity of gods and idols, in the same way that Greece and Rome had many gods that coexisted and served a common purpose.

In Silicon Valley, where much of modern technology is invented, many of the inventors are having attacks of conscience. Like the creators of the atom bomb during WWII, they worry that their inventions may lead to the destruction of the world. This angst is producing high levels of stress, lots of anxiety and many sleepless nights. However, when people are troubled like this, instead of turning to Christianity, the Bible or even psychology, they instead turn to Eastern religions to soothe their troubled soul.

Esalen Institute

Since the Esalen Institute in Big Sur, California was repurposed in 2018 to serve Silicon Valley, it has been fully booked ever since. In 1962, Esalen was originally founded as the nation's first gateway to Eastern religion, and in particular, to the practice of Yoga. Called the "hippie hotel" at the time, people checked in from all over America to experience nude therapy sessions and Yoga meditation. Esalen is flatly credited with bringing such meditation into the American mainstream.[220] It thrived until May 2017 when massive mudslides on the California coast cut off all access to the outside world. It was during this time of isolation that

---

220 *The New York Times*, "Where Silicon Valley Is Going To Get In Touch With Its Soul", Nellie Bowles, December 4, 2017.

the Esalen facility was rejuvenated and restructured for Silicon Valley elites.[221] Its mission has been expanded from the personal to social awareness as described by one San Jose, CA. newspaper:

> *Perched on a rocky promontory above the pounding Pacific surf, the 54-year-old nonprofit will still offer classes in breathing, yoga, chanting, tantric sex and meditation. But it will also hold workshops like "Greater Good" and "Dancing with the Planetary Crisis," about technology and sustainability. It has created space for experimental new programs, yet unnamed. And in the future, it will offer global online access to once-exclusive events.*[222]

Some of these new programs include the *Connect to Your Inner-Net* workshop, which is described on Esalen's website:

> *How can the modern workplace become a source of inner peace and* **global transformation***? During this workshop, Mirabai Bush and Gopi Kallayil will explore why and how organizations such as Google teach mindfulness and emotional intelligence skills and offer yoga programs at work. These wellness initiatives are offered through innovative experiential learning programs such as Search Inside Yourself (SIY) and Yoglers. The SIY curriculum and methodology is based on the realization that the solutions to many of our problems lie within ourselves, and that by practicing mindfulness at work, we can become more emotionally intelligent, recover from adversity more easily and swiftly, and create possibilities for ourselves and our organizations to flourish. Building on these ideas and best practices,* **participants can learn how to create a community of mindfulness in their workplaces.**

> *Participants will be taught contemplative practices including methods designed for the workplace, like mindful emailing and mindful listening. At work,* **these methods have been shown to enhance mental fitness and clarity, develop agile and adaptive mindsets, reduce stress responses, increase resilience, enhance creativity, develop greater self-awareness and communication skills, and increase**

---

221 NPR, "'Lifeline' Stretch Of California's Highway 1 Reopens 14 Months After Massive Mudslide", Amy Held, July 18, 2018.
222 *The Mercury News*, "Esalen's survival story: A tale of transformation", Lisa Krieger, July 21, 2017.

overall well-being. *This workshop is designed for individuals and also for workplace managers.*[223] [emphasis added]

Other workshops offered include:

The Future of Money: The Role of Blockchain and Cryptocurrency

- Dance of Oneness®: Rumi and the Dance of Light
- The Wild Woman's Way: Embodied Feminine Practice
- Heart to Heart: 5Rhythms® Heartbeat and Buddhist Heart Practice
- Self-compassion, Joy and Loving Kindness through Meditation and Iyengar Yoga[224]

Throughout the Eastern flair at Esalen, Hinduism, Buddhism, Zen Buddhism and Taoism, among others, proliferate. Anything of a Christian or Judeo/Christian ethic is pointedly excluded and disallowed.

Burning Man

On August 25, 2018, 75,000 devotees descended on the Black Rock Desert in northern Nevada to experience the so-called Burning Man. Collectively, they create and inhabit Black Rock City until September 3 when it is completely dismantled and the desert floor is scraped clean. Burners hate to be called a festival because it is much more than that. It is primal, evolutionary, spontaneous, inclusive, hedonistic and unexpected. It is the beginning and the ending. Anything goes at Burning Man, as long as it is not patently illegal. Having started in 1986, this was the 33rd annual gathering.

The 10 principles that give structure to Burning Man must be agreed to by every attendee before entering Black Rock City:

Radical Inclusion - *Anyone may be a part of Burning Man. We welcome and respect the stranger. No prerequisites exist for participation in our community.*

---

223 See workshop at Esalen.org, "Connect to Your Inner-Net: Mindful Practices for Life and Work", October 26-28, 2018.
224 See Esalen.org/Learn for more information

Gifting - *Burning Man is devoted to acts of gift giving. The value of a gift is unconditional. Gifting does not contemplate a return or an exchange for something of equal value.*

Decommodification - *In order to preserve the spirit of gifting, our community seeks to create social environments that are unmediated by commercial sponsorships, transactions, or advertising. We stand ready to protect our culture from such exploitation. We resist the substitution of consumption for participatory experience.*

Radical Self-reliance - *Burning Man encourages the individual to discover, exercise and rely on his or her inner resources.*

Radical Self-expression - *Radical self-expression arises from the unique gifts of the individual. No one other than the individual or a collaborating group can determine its content. It is offered as a gift to others. In this spirit, the giver should respect the rights and liberties of the recipient.*

Communal Effort - *Our community values creative cooperation and collaboration. We strive to produce, promote and protect social networks, public spaces, works of art, and methods of communication that support such interaction.*

Civic Responsibility - *We value civil society. Community members who organize events should assume responsibility for public welfare and endeavor to communicate civic responsibilities to participants. They must also assume responsibility for conducting events in accordance with local, state and federal laws.*

Leaving No Trace - *Our community respects the environment. We are committed to leaving no physical trace of our activities wherever we gather. We clean up after ourselves and endeavor, whenever possible, to leave such places in a better state than when we found them.*

Participation - *Our community is committed to a radically participatory ethic. We believe that transformative change, whether in the individual or in society, can occur only through the medium of deeply personal participation. We achieve being through doing. Everyone is invited to work. Everyone is* *invited to play. We make the world real through actions that open the heart.*

Immediacy - *Immediate experience is, in many ways, the most important touchstone of value in our culture. We seek to overcome barriers that stand between us and a recognition of our inner selves, the reality of those around us, participation in society, and contact with a natural world exceeding human powers. No idea can substitute for this experience.*[225]

Outside of these, anything goes and indeed, it does! One Burning Man insider wrote,

It is our palette and canvas, to create the world we can't enjoy at home... it's pagan. It's anti-religious. It's a Trojan horse... It's a chance to get out of town and hang with some good chaps. It's sex and drugs and trance music. It's artistic expression. It's a week of survival on chips and salsa... It's Utopia-On-A-Stick.[226]

According to one 2018 attendee, it is a platform to explore alternative spiritualities.[227] After the 2017 Burn, co-founder Larry Harvey elaborated on that year's theme, *Radical Ritual*:

The whole point, this year, was to convince people that Burning Man is a spiritual movement. It's not a religion, but it's a spiritual movement. And you know it when you see it.[228]

Yes, spiritual. Burning Man is chocked full of Yoga, Buddhism, Hinduism, shamanism, goddess rituals, sacred femininity, tarot, satanism, vodou, ancient deities and just about every other flavor of cultic and occultic thought imaginable. It is the melting pot of the religious universe and the new headquarters for the worship of man-made idols.

This is also where Silicon Valley goes to invent itself. When Google was incorporated on September 4, 1998, the team was already busy setting up at Burning Man. Their offices were artistically decorated with Burning Man images and the company

---

225 See BurningMan.org website, "The 10 Principles of Burning Man".
226 S. McKenzie, "Utopia-On-A-Stick", September 3, 1998, as quoted by Game of Gods, Carl Teichrib, 2018, p. 520.
227 Ibid., p. 523..
228 Ibid. p. 524

ran a free shuttle-bus to the event.[229] When Google hired its first outside CEO, Eric Schmidt, it was largely on the basis that he was a fellow Burner. The world has never been the same since.

Other avid Burners include Big Tech leaders like Sergey Brin and Larry Page (Google), Jeff Bezos (Amazon), Elon Musk (Tesla), Dustin Moskovitz and Justin Rosenstein (Asana), Mark Zuckerberg (Facebook), Garrett Camp (Uber), Alexis Ohanian (Reddit), Drew Houston (Dropbox), plus a host of venture capitalists and wannabes from all walks of life, hoping for some kind of a big break. Indeed, Burning Man is *the* networking event of the year for all of Silicon Valley and its extended families.

Harkening back to the 2017/2018 recreation of Esalen in Big Sur, The *Mercury News* reported that "volunteers from Burning Man pulled weeds, cut trees and repaired eroded landscapes."[230] This was more than just a nice gesture between 'birds of a feather': it was a labor of love to perpetuate the spiritualized culture.

In short, the *Utopia-On-A-Stick* is whatever one wants to make of it. Many have noted that there is no room for conservative thought, but it is not necessarily because attendees are not conservative. It would also be an error to call them leftists, communists, socialists or even fascists. Rather, they are Technocrats who hold to a narrow vision of Utopia run by technology, AI, robotics, etc. Anyone who will not get in line with this vision is marginalized or excluded. Are you with them or against them? The evidence of loyalty is based on worshipping at the right altar, as long it is found at the likes of Esalen or Burning Man.

The Church of AI

Anthony Levandowski, a Burner and former engineer with Google and Uber, founded the first church of AI in 2017, called the *Way of the Future* (WOTF). AI is its god to be worshipped. According to *Wired*:

---

229 Ibid., p. 518.
230 Op Cit.

WOTF's activities will focus on "the realization, acceptance, and worship of a Godhead based on Artificial Intelligence (AI) developed through computer hardware and software." That includes funding research to help create the divine AI itself. The religion will seek to build working relationships with AI industry leaders and create a membership through community outreach, initially targeting AI professionals and "laypersons who are interested in the worship of a Godhead based on AI."

"What is going to be created will effectively be a god," Levandowski tells me in his modest mid-century home on the outskirts of Berkeley, California. "It's not a god in the sense that it makes lightning or causes hurricanes. But if there is something a billion times smarter than the smartest human, what else are you going to call it?"[231]

The influence of Burning Man can be seen in WOTF, but Levandowski is the first person to actually turn AI into a god to be worshipped. At least, it makes sense to add it to the other gods represented at Burning Man.

Green Religion

If Burners are building the Utopia of Technocracy, they are still a very small minority compared to the whole world. We have already demonstrated that Sustainable Development, aka Technocracy, is a global movement with hundreds of millions of avid followers. Although there are other Burning Man type events around the world, they still only touch a fraction of the population. Are the established religions of these masses simply ignored? Hardly.

Unfortunately, almost all Christian denominations have abandoned historical teachings based on the Bible and have turned enmass to Sustainable Development and what is known as 'green theology'.

231 *Wired*, "Inside the First Church of Artificial Intelligence", Michelle Le, November 15, 2017.

The World Council of Churches (WCC), for instance, represents 349 member denominations, which collectively represent over 560 million members in 110 nations. The WCC is a leader in the global Interfaith movement and was a signatory to the UN-inspired Earth Charter. The WCC held the Interfaith Summit on Climate Change in September 2014. Rev. Dr. Serene Jones, president of Union Theological Seminary echoed a familiar sentiment of Burning Man:

> *Now is the time for us to come together across divisive issues and divergent traditions and use our reach and influence for the good of the earth we share."*[232]

After the summit, the Executive Director of GreenFaith, Rev. David Fletcher, recapped his excitement:

> *There has never been such a large amount of religious-environmental activity in one location in the history of the world. This week will mark a watershed in the history of religion. It will be the time that people remember as **the time when the world's faiths declared themselves, irrevocably, as green faiths.**[233]* [emphasis added]

The Roman Catholic church claims 1.2 billion members worldwide. In May 2015, Pope Francis issued his infamous *Laudato si'*, also known as the *Encyclical on Environment and Human Ecology*. The Encyclical was viewed by many Catholics as a complete sell-out to the United Nations, global warming and Sustainable Development. The Encyclical was fully clarified shortly thereafter in a statement to the United Nations delivered by Archbishop Bernardito Auza:

> *We support the verbatim inclusion of the sustainable development goals and targets as in the Report of the OWG (Open Working Group)." Toward the end of the statement, the Archbishop added, "We would strongly encourage the use*

---

232 *Huffington Post*, "For the Good of Our Shared Earth: The World Council of Churches", September 10, 2014.
233 Ibid.

and coordination of all sources of financing to achieve the
SDGs and development in general.[234]

The Muslim faith has some 1.8 billion adherents, making up
approximately 24% of world population. Concepts of environmentalism, Sustainable Development and Green Economy are
deeply embedded into the Quran, where approximately 750 of its
6236 verses (12 percent) refer to "various aspects of nature, the
relationship between man and nature, vegetal and animal organ-
isms and their environment."[235] In fact, the Quran is the only religious book that has doctrines of environmentalism embedded
into its core doctrines.

In his book, *Green Deen*, author Ibrahim Abdul-Matin explains
that the Arabic meaning of the word "Deen" is "way" or "path."
Thus, Islam is proposed as the "Green Way". An environmentalist,
he explains that "Islam is what motivates me to be a steward of
the Earth."[236] His text then takes him into the same dogma pro-
liferated by the United Nations: Smart Grid, water management,
poverty reduction, green jobs, food security and alternative energy. He states that "energy from hell is energy that is derived
from the ground" and that it "disturbs the balance (mizan) of the
universe and is therefore a great injustice (zulum)."[237] In replacement, Abdul-Matin suggests that "energy from heaven comes from
above. It is not extracted from the Earth, and it is renewable."[238]
His religious zeal for earth is aptly summarized by a single statement: "The Earth is a mosque, and everything in it is sacred."[239]

There is no reason to belabor the point. Humans are spiritual
creatures and will always find something to worship, and postmodern society is no exception to any period that preceded us.
One thing should be bluntly clear: Like the tumblers in a combination lock, all the major religions of the world are lined up to

---

234 Lepanto Institute, "Vatican Representative Endorses UN Sustainable Development Goals,
'Varbatim'".
235 Lucrările Seminarului Geografic "Dimitrie Cantemir" NR. 42, "Environmental Education in the Holy
Quran", 2016, pp. 157-163.
236 Green Deen, Ibrahim Abdul-Matin (Kube Publishing, 2012), p.3.
237 Ibid. p. 77.
238 Ibid. p. 89.
239 Ibid. p. 3.

simultaneously worship the earth and the environment, and they are all supporting the core doctrines of the United Nations.

CHAPTER 11

RESISTANCE IS NEVER FUTILE

Eternal vigilance is the price of liberty.[228]

In the late 1970s, when Professor Antony Sutton and I were speaking extensively about the Trilateral Commission and its globalist policies, we touched hundreds of thousands of Americans with a warning about globalization. Our books, *Trilaterals Over Washington, Volumes I and II*, were widely circulated and some even found their way into university classrooms. We publicly debated members of the Trilateral Commission in person and on radio, and we were interviewed on over 300 radio stations across the nation; the pinnacle of our media activity was a live three-hour debate on the Larry King overnight radio program on Mutual Broadcasting Network, between myself and the Executive Director of the Trilateral Commission, Charles Heck.

On one hand, we received very positive feedback from everyone we met. Yes, they understood. Yes, they agreed. However, nothing really changed. When President Ronald Reagan was inaugurated in 1981, previously-alarmed Americans retreated to their living rooms assuming that "the Gipper" would put a halt to Trilateral

---

228 Inscribed on the statue at the right side of the main entrance to the National Archives of the United States, Washington, D.C.

Commission nonsense and hence, globalization. What they didn't take into consideration was that Vice-President George H.W. Bush was himself a member of the Trilateral Commission. Neither did they realize that after the George H.W. Bush administration, Bill Clinton and Al Gore, both members of the Trilateral Commission, continued Commission policies that led to the total entrenchment of globalization.

The dilemma is this: merely warning of the trouble to come was not enough to mount resistance to oppose it. I suggest that this phenomenon be named *"Sutton's Paradox"*, in honor of the world-class researcher who saw early-on what the consequences of globalization would be. It seems intuitive that such accurate warnings of this type would elicit a positive response. If a child reaches for a hot stove and the parent loudly proclaims "Don't touch it. That will burn you!", you expect the child to retract his hand. If you warn occupants of a burning house to get out, you expect that they will exit immediately. Thus, we might expect the Warning-Action dynamic to be universally true, but it is not! Sutton's Paradox could be succinctly stated as, "The degree of personal response is inversely proportional to the length of time to personal pain."

The obvious problem with this phenomenon is that over the last 45 years, globalization has had free reign to embed itself throughout the world at all levels of society. With our early warnings fully materialized, we are now thoroughly entangled with globalization and vice versa. However, today's discussions about globalization elicit a different response from ordinary citizens: "It's too big, and there is nothing we can do to stop it."

When I discovered historic Technocracy and related it to the Trilateral Commission's *New International Economic Order*, it quickly led to additional warnings with the publishing of my book *Technocracy Rising: The Trojan Horse of Global Transformation* in December 2014 and the creation of the web journal, *Technocracy News & Trends*. Today's warnings are definitely more granular and personal than they were in 1980 with the advent of massive surveillance, Smart Grid, 5G, Internet of Things, property rights abuses, etc. Unfortunately, Sutton's Paradox is still alive and well as people sit back and expect someone else to save them. [229]

Further insight into Sutton's Paradox is necessary. For the most part, it seems that people's actions are only selfish and self-focused. In other words, action is prompted by personally felt pain. If there is no personal pain, there is no action. The pain that your neighbor feels is irrelevant to any possible action on your part to stop it, unless is it an immediate life-or-death situation like a house fire. Furthermore, societal pain can be well described and alarming, but it just isn't a motivation for personal action.

This may seem like a harsh assessment, but America's decline has been enabled by the persistent and near-sighted selfishness of its citizens to avoid doing anything to stop it. We have been amply educated, and pointedly warned and there has even been general agreement on the risks and dangers, but it hasn't produced the necessary backlash.

The opposite of selfishness is selflessness. Collins Dictionary defines selfless as "devoted to others' welfare or interests and not one's own; unselfish; altruistic; self-sacrificing." Being selfless means the giving of time, money or things to others without looking for immediate personal gain. It means doing what is right simply because it is the right thing to do even in the face of personal inconvenience or loss.

Acting in a selfless manner doesn't automatically define the moral reason for doing so. Communism, Socialism, Marxism and Fascism all tricked their subjects into abandoning selfishness and acting selflessly, or "for the cause and not the self." This is also the greatest fallacy of collectivism, where individual rights are sacrificed for the greater good, however that "good" might be defined.

On the positive side, we can thank the selfless behavior of the Founding Fathers who put everything on the line for the Declaration of Independence and the Constitution. It was selfless soldiers who fought numerous wars to keep America free. Selfless behavior can be seen daily through numerous "random acts of

---

229 Note: The "Reagan will save us" mentality of the 1980s has been replaced with "Trump will save us".

kindness" and "pay it forward" charity. All of these demonstrate that while selfless behavior is a choice, its outcome depends on the moral compass from which it emanates. This was made clear from the beginning of our nation by multiple Founding Fathers. For instance, John Adams wrote,

> *Our Constitution was made only for a moral and religious people. It is wholly inadequate to the government of any other.*

Edmund Burke echoed this sentiment:

> *Men are qualified for civil liberty in exact proportion to their disposition to put moral chains upon their appetites.*

The earlier statement, "It's too big and there is nothing we can do to stop it" is the thoroughly selfish approach towards today's problems. Whether or not it can be stopped is irrelevant; simply put, morality demands that we do the right thing simply because it is the right thing to do, not because we might fail or be denied some personal gain.

In short, resistance to evil, evildoing and evildoers should be a moral imperative regardless of personal or societal obstacles. *It is never wrong to do the right thing!*

Thinking back to 1978-1981, very few, if any, would have imagined or approved of the future we have today. When warned of this possibility, they did nothing to resist it. If they had tried and failed, there would be no blame, but failing to try is a failure of our basic sense of morality. To reiterate, responsible and selfless Americans act because it is the right thing to do, and this is the challenge before us.

But, there is another aspect of our collective failure that must be faced. There have been many thousands of selfless patriots over the years who have worked tirelessly to stem the tide of America's decline. They have given of their time and money, some at great personal cost, to fight against the forces of darkness that would destroy America. However, this begs the question: Given their great effort, why is America worse off today than ever before?

Since this writer has been both an observer and participant for over 40 years, my stark observation is that we have been fighting the wrong enemy. We have been outsmarted by a clever enemy to draw us into meaningless fights while they continue on unseen and unopposed. This enemy has waged war according to the timeless principles of the ancient Chinese General Sun Tzu who penned *The Art of War* over 2,500 years ago. The evidence and cause of our failure is deduced from this exhortation:

If you know yourself but not the enemy, for every victory gained you will also suffer a defeat. If you know neither the enemy nor yourself, you will succumb in every battle.[230]

At the very least, this means we have not adequately known the enemy and in some cases, we have not known ourselves. But, the enemy has known us and created a successful strategy against us:

Therefore the skillful leader subdues the enemy's troops without any fighting; he captures their cities without laying siege to them; he overthrows their kingdom without lengthy operations in the field. With his forces intact he will dispute the mastery of the Empire, and thus, without losing a man, his triumph will be complete. **This is the method of attacking by stratagem.**[231] [emphasis added]

Could it be that Richard Gardner was thinking about this in 1974 when he wrote,

The 'house of world order' will have to be built from the bottom up rather than from the top down..., **an end run around national sovereignty, eroding it piece by piece, will accomplish much more than the old-fashioned frontal assault...** [232] [emphasis added]

What is Effective Resistance?

American liberty and freedom have never been under such a sustained assault politically, economically and socially. The very fabric of our nation is being torn apart and many opposing

---

230 Sun-tzu, and Samuel B. Griffith, *The Art of War*, [Oxford: Clarendon Press, 1964], p.11.
231 Ibid., p. 9.
232 Richard N. Gardner, *The Hard Road to World Order*, Foreign Affairs, April 1974.

groups seem to be irreconcilable. While a national approach to stopping this battle was appropriate in the 1970s, it is wholly inappropriate today. Why? Because Sustainable Development was just a plan that had been conceived but not yet birthed. When the United Nations' Agenda 21 was revealed in 1992, a combination of national and state-level resistance might have been sufficient to scuttle the operation, but alas, America missed that opportunity as well.

In the 26 years since 1992, the policies of Sustainable Development, Agenda 21, 2030 Agenda and New Urban Agenda have taken root in every local community in America. As we have already seen, this assault on local communities bypassed national and state barriers under the mantra "Think global, act local." In addition, regional governance organizations[233] have quietly usurped sovereignty from cities and counties for the specific reason to implement these policies outside the purview of duly elected representatives.

This has moved the battle line down to our own local communities, where personal and local action offers the only possibility for effective pushback. The Federal government is not in any position to clean up your community and neither is your state government. Thus, it is up to local citizens to take charge in their own communities if there is to be any effective resistance. In a broad sense, this implies a gargantuan movement. In the local sense, any group of dedicated citizens can achieve tangible results right where they are, but only if they follow the shrewd principles of *The Art of War*:

- **Know your enemy** - e.g., do your homework, research and thorough investigation *before* you lift a finger to engage.
- **Make correct self-assessment** - "Carefully compare the opposing army with your own, so that you may

---

[233] Note: this includes Councils of Governments (COGS), Metropolitan Planning Organizations (MPOS) and Smart Regions.

know where strength is superabundant and where it is deficient"[234]

- **Create a strategy** - "All men can see the tactics whereby I conquer, but what none can see is the strategy out of which victory is evolved."[235]

- **Keep your mouth shut!** - "O divine art of subtlety and secrecy! Through you we learn to be invisible, through you inaudible; and hence we can hold the enemy's fate in our hands."[236] Everything you say on any public social media platform is *immediately* known by your opponents!

- **Then Just do it!** - "Let your plans be dark and impenetrable as night, and when you move, fall like a thunderbolt."[237]

After finding some like-minded people to work with, make a general survey of your entire community. Note all agencies and boards (education, water, fire, law enforcement, etc.), leaders, locations, meetings, contact information and websites. Make a list of any and all initiatives that you can spot, their purpose, progress and people involved. Make an assessment of every person you encounter in order to locate some who might be favorable to your cause or position.

Next, pick a couple of upcoming local meetings to attend and just go to find out what they are like. Simply observe, don't speak. Watch the personalities, pick up on strategies or tactics used, listen for hidden agendas, note the bosses and the followers. Also note audience members and any role they might be playing.

If you do these few things, you will be ready to choose an area of involvement.

---

234 Ibid., p. 22.
235 Ibid., p. 23.
236 Ibid., p.20.
237 Ibid., p. 27.

Tools that help

Meeting with your group frequently and in person is essential to any action plan. Don't meet in public, but rather in someone's home or office. Keep it private.

Electronic communication is necessary to coordinate certain things, but let's use our head here. Don't *ever* use Gmail, Facebook, Twitter or other public utilities. Don't make phone calls on open carriers that can be surveilled. In place of those, here are some excellent replacement tools.

Secure email - Check out Proton Mail (ProtonMail.com), StartMail (StartMail.com) and HushMail (HushMail.com) for starters. They all have secure, end-to-end encryption and nobody can read your email except the intended recipients. If messages are stored on a server, they are still fully encrypted and unreadable.

Text Messaging and Phone Calls - Signal (Signal.org) is the only encrypted chat and phone service endorsed by Edward Snowden. There are free Apps that work on any smartphone as well as on your computer. Signal never stores text messages on a server, but rather encrypts and delivers every message directly to the addressee. Furthermore, you can make fully-encrypted, end-to-end phone calls to other Signal users; this means no eavesdropping and no offline storage. Encrypted phone calls are critical considering that every major carrier can store and transcribe your phone calls. Other encrypted apps include SilentPhone (SilentCircle.com), and BBM (bbm.com); yes, this is BlackBerry Messenger!

Browsing - Use only a secure browser that does not save the history of sites you visit. When searching, do not use a search engine that saves your searches. Safe search engines include DuckDuckGo.com and StartPage.com. Safe browsers are Opera.com, Brave.com and EpicBrowser.com. The latter two include free access to a Virtual Private Network for even more privacy.

Social media - Don't say anything on Facebook, Twitter, Google, Instagram, etc. Professional analytics companies use sophisticated data mining algorithms to know everything about you and they eagerly sell your data to anyone who will pay. The less you say, the better, but *never* reveal anything about your strategies, fellow activists, etc. However, given the demonstrated value of social media and its potential for teamwork and collaboration, we have created an alternative private and encrypted social media platform called LocalActivist (LocalActivist.org). It is ONLY for local activists or those who are ready to step up to the plate to take action. New members are carefully screened and 100 percent of the site is encrypted and protected on private servers. If you create Groups on LocalActivist, you can invite your team to join and then exchange messages, files, links, events, pictures, etc., without fear of data-mining or snoops.

Success Stories From the Front Lines

You will never hear of any local activist success stories in the mainstream media because all such stories are automatically embargoed (i.e., spiked). But can you imagine that there are such success stories out there?

In Great Britain, citizens prevailed in court to override the Gateshead Council's use of fraudulent and incorrect data upon which to make decisions about 5G in that community. The judge concluded, "The public has a right to know."[238]

In the sleepy community of Santa Maria Tonantzintla, Mexico, local citizens got wind of a Smart City makeover that would literally change the nature of their town. The citizens organized and after finding flaws in the permitting process, they told the unwanted planners to get out of town.[239]

In Hesperia, California, local activists went after Agenda 21 policies and ultimately got a 5 to 0 vote of the City Council to overturn and rescind the Countywide Vision statement that had been endorsed in 2011. This was a major undertaking by local

---

238 *SmombieGate*, "Britain's First 5G Court Case And The People Won", October 10, 2018.
239 *The Guardian*, "The Mexican Town That Refused To Become A Smart City", October 16, 2018.

citizens, but through patience and persistence they prevailed and delivered a major setback to California's Smart City planners.[240]

Mill Valley is a wealthy city of 14,000 just north of San Francisco, California. Citizens sent 145 pieces of correspondence voicing their opposition to the proposed implementation of 5G, citing health and safety concerns. The City Council voted unanimously to block 5G deployment of 5G wireless towers in the city's residential areas.[241]

In Arizona, a pilot program for vaccine education was completely scuttled by just 120 individuals and parents. The spokesman for the Arizona Department of Health Services, Brenda Jones, said afterward, "We're so sorry we couldn't make a go of this — strong forces against us."[242] Strong forces? Indeed! The power of local citizens is immense when focused and used wisely.

Note that all of these victories are within 90 days of the publication of this book! There were many more just like them. In each case, only a few local citizen activists made the difference. Patience and persistence paid off.

In short, these victories are very compelling because if they can do it, *so can you! Resistance is never futile.*

240 *iAgenda 21*, "Hesperia, California: 5 – 0 Victory to Rescind the San Bernardino County Countywide Vision Achieved", October 3, 2018.
241 *TechCrunch*, "Bay Area city blocks 5G deployments over cancer concerns", September 30, 2018.
242 *AZ Central*, "Arizona cancels vaccine program after backlash from parents who don't vaccinate", October 18, 2018.

Chapter 12

Conclusion

Because sentence against an evil work is not executed speedily, therefore the heart of the sons of men is fully set in them to do evil. - Ecclesiastes 8:11

The ebb and flow of history is never a straight line. If this book has presented too much of a linear explanation of the way things are, how we arrived to this point, and why, then we must temper our understanding with the complexity of human existence. The world has many lines of demarcation that can lead to conflict; some cultures are radically different and will not mix well; some political systems are irreconcilable with others; some economic realities cannot be reconciled. Most importantly, the temperament of man is unpredictable, leading some to be peaceable, some to fight, some to steal and others to kill.

All of these forces move forward while colliding, intermixing and influencing each other, like a mesmerizing swirl of bright paint poured onto the artist's canvas. It may appear as chaos, as Richard Gardner suggested with his "booming, buzzing reality" comment.

This complexity is what makes it impossible to clearly foresee the future in great detail, but at any given moment we are well suited to identify and examine major trends to see what direction we are headed, at what speed and who is trying to steer the ship. Some men have done very well at this, like Aldous Huxley in *Brave New World* or George Orwell in *Nineteen Eighty-Four*. Huxley painted a scientific dictatorship that relied on pleasure to control the citizenry; Orwell used pain. Were both wrong? No, but neither were they 100 percent right. However, people today can read both books and clearly see that they had a lot of things right.

The spirit of this book is to paint a larger picture than you might be used to looking at. It is to raise your elevation so that you can see a broader horizon. It is to reveal mega-trends along with the history of what started and what drives them on.

Throughout history, every generation of man has had to struggle through pretty much the same dilemma. If they didn't like their present conditions, they had to figure out ways to improve their lot. Worse, if they didn't like the future they saw coming, they had to take steps to try and change it. Some generations succeeded. Others failed miserably.

This book exposes many trends, forces, organizations and people that are steering the world toward scientific dictatorship and neo-Feudalism. Most of mankind will ignorantly follow the flow, waking up in a very bad place one day and wondering how they got there.

Huxley's *Brave New World* (1932) was creepy but brilliant, looking straight into the face of budding Technocracy that resided at Columbia University in the same year. He simply let his mind run with it, extrapolating ideas to their logical ends. Few people know that Huxley followed up in 1958 with an non-fiction update appropriately called *Brave New World Revisited*. The 28 year span between these two books gave Huxley plenty of time to rethink his analysis, predictions and conclusions. What started as fiction in 1932 was morphing into reality by 1958. This seemed to somewhat unnerve him as he wrote:

> *The older dictators fell because they could never supply their subjects with enough bread, enough circuses, enough miracles and mysteries. Nor did they possess a really effective system of mind-manipulation. In the past, free-thinkers and revolutionaries were often the products of the most pi-*

*ously orthodox education. This is not surprising. The methods
employed by orthodox educators were and still are extremely
inefficient. Under a scientific dictator education will really
work -- with the result that most men and women will grow
up to love their servitude and will never dream of revolution.*
***There seems to be no good reason why a thoroughly sci-
entific dictatorship should ever be overthrown.***[233] [em-
phasis added]

In other words, he not only saw scientific dictatorship more
clearly but also realized that if it ever were to become firmly established, it would be "game over" for humanity, without hope for
an overthrow.

On this point, I agree with Huxley.

It took hundreds of years to develop the concepts of freedom
and liberty that resulted in the founding of America in 1776.
Scientific Dictatorship is the polar opposite of such freedom and
liberty, and yet it can potentially be cemented into place within a
few decades. If Technocracy succeeds, it could take hundreds of
additional years to relight the flame. It is for this reason that the
stakes are so astronomically high in how we respond to this clear
and present danger.

I must state neither Aldous Huxley or his brother, Julian, were
heroes of mine. They were globalists, humanists, eugenicists and
atheists. Julian Huxley was the first Director of UNESCO, president of the British Humanist Association and a founding member of the World Wildlife fund; he was also a long-time member
of the British Eugenics Society and served as its president from
1959-1962. Indeed, the Huxleys contributed more to our modern
condition than most other global elitists of their day.

Having said that, Huxley's closing paragraph in *Revisited* can
be taken with a grain of salt. His moral being might have been
radically different than our own, but we still might agree with his
prescient conclusion, at least for our own purposes:

*Meanwhile there is still some freedom left in the world. Many
young people, it is true, do not seem to value freedom. But*

233 Aldous Huxley, Brave New World REvisited, [1958, Harper & Brothers], p. 147.

some of us still believe that, without freedom, human beings
cannot become fully human and that freedom is therefore su-
premely valuable. Perhaps the forces that now menace free-
dom are too strong to be resisted for very long. It is still our
duty to do whatever we can to resist them.[234]

We must also close the loop on Zbigniew Brzezinski's book,
Between Two Ages: America's Role in the Technetronic Era.
Remember that it was this 1970 book that inspired industrial-
ist/banker David Rockefeller to invite Brzezinski to become a
co-founder of the Trilateral Commission in 1973 where he also
served as the first Executive Director. An academic to the core,
nothing Brzezinski ever wrote was easy to understand, but there
are a few noteworthy thoughts that clearly stand out.

Brzezinski had much to say about revolutionary movements
and forces. The fact that he wrote about being between two different ages means that there were actually three ages in view: the
one in the middle and the ones on either end. When he wrote the
book, it was during the middle age and he was looking forward
to the final Technetronic Era sometime in the future. Now, that
future has arrived and we can judge how well he pegged it.

Although he explored multiple scenarios, one picked up on the
"gradual appearance of a more controlled and directed society"[235]
when he wrote:

Such a society would be dominated by an elite whose claim
to political power would rest on allegedly superior scientific
know-how. Unhindered by the restraints of traditional liberal
values, this elite would not hesitate to achieve its political
ends by using the latest modern techniques for influencing
public behavior and keeping society under close surveillance
and control. Under such circumstances, the scientific and
technological momentum of the country would not be re-
versed but would actually feed on the situation it exploits.[236]

This was the start of a much broader exploration of what the
Technetronic era could look like:

---

234 Ibid.
235 Zbigniew Brzezinski, *Between Two Ages*, [1970, Viking Press], p.252.
236 Ibid. p. 253.

Persisting social crisis, the emergence of a charismatic personality, and the exploitation of mass media to obtain public confidence would be the stepping stones in the piecemeal transformation of the United States into a highly controlled society.[237]

His "piecemeal transformation" suspiciously echoes the sentiment of Richard Gardner's "end run around national sovereignty", but goes further to refine the endgame of a "highly controlled society." However, the similarities don't end here.

Brzezinski was blunt about his disdain for America and its Constitution when he wrote:

*The approaching two-hundredth anniversary of the Declaration of Independence could justify the call for a **national constitutional convention to re-examine the nation's formal institutional framework.** Either 1976 or 1989 - the two-hundredth anniversary of the Constitution - could serve as a suitable target date for culminating a national dialogue on the relevance of existing arrangements, the workings of the representative process, and the desirability of initiating various European regionalization reforms and of streamlining the administrative structure. More important still, either date would provide a suitable occasion for **redefining the meaning of modern democracy.**[238]* [emphasis added]

The fact that Brzezinski made this call for a constitutional convention in 1970 should provide great alarm to all those who are demanding such a convention today![239]

*Realism, however, forces us to recognize that the necessary political innovation will not come from direct constitutional reform, desirable as that would be. **The needed change is more likely to develop incrementally and less overtly.** Nonetheless, its eventual scope may be far-reaching, especially as the political process gradually assimilates scientific-technological change... The trend toward more coordination*

---

237 Ibid.
238 Ibid., p. 259.
239 Note: Trilateral Commission member Henry Kissinger likewise called for a constitutional convention in the early 1970s.

but less centralization would be in keeping with the American tradition of blurring sharp distinctions between public and private institutions.[240] [emphasis added]

When examining Richard Gardner's exact phrase, one can sense just how positionally aligned he was to Brzezinski:

*It will look like a great "booming, buzzing confusion," but **an end-run around national sovereignty, eroding it piece by piece,** will accomplish much more than the old-fashioned frontal assault.*[241] [emphasis added]

All other things, forces and factors aside, there have been several touchstones that always keep Trilateral-style globalization, aka Technocracy and Sustainable Development, on track. Like a pool table in chaos when the first rack of balls is broken with a hard-hit cue ball, the players never lose sight that the goal is to get every ball into one of the designated pockets. Some of these bedrock goals include:

- Erase America's Constitutional Republic form of government - it stands in the way of "progress".
- Take all land and water resources away from individuals and governments - this is the source of all wealth on earth, regardless of monetary systems.
- Crush Capitalism and Free Enterprise once and for all - Capitalism is incompatible with Sustainable Development and puts too much wealth in the hands of citizens.
- Establish energy as the core economic mediator - it is the lifeblood of Sustainable Development.
- Always use available science and technology to accomplish the above - it's the easiest and quickest way to fool and control the maximum number of people.
- Use incremental transformations (end-runs) rather than frontal attacks - this minimizes any possible resistance.

---

240 Ibid., p. 260.
241 *Foreign Affairs*, Vol. 52, Number 3, 1974, pp 557-576..

Stress to Distress

Everyone has an explanation as to why society is trending toward chaos. Intolerance, hatred, violence, racial tensions, crime and fear are the new normal, and people are compulsively looking to one group or another to blame. However, their horizon is too low. Over the last 50 years, the global elite have been very masterful at posing, orchestrating and then inflaming conflicts to drive people to ground level where they can only see the immediate "enemy". As long as a person has a suitable and plausible enemy to lash out toward, there will be no further effort to locate the real enemy.

When David Rockefeller and Zbigniew Brzezinski started the Trilateral Commission in 1973, they were very strategic about covering their tracks. President Jimmy Carter and Vice President Walter Mondale were both members of the Trilateral Commission - Democrats, right? Then Ronald Reagan chose George H.W. Bush. - Republicans, right? Both Bill Clinton and Vice president Al Gore were Trilaterals. Oops, back to Democrats, right? Then George W. Bush chose his Vice President in Dick Cheney. President Obama, a Democrat, was surrounded by members of the Trilateral Commission. So, who is the enemy? Democrat or Republican?

Obviously, the answer is neither. Both parties have been played as stooges for a public audience looking for someone to blame for their woes. Regardless of who gets elected, it's just business as usual for the elite handlers who have been morphing the economic system into Technocracy.

Why is society nearing chaos? Because it is the natural and obvious outcome of this transformation. Richard Gardner saw it coming in 1974 as a "booming, buzzing confusion".

When education has been horrifically dumbed down for multiple generations so that critical thinking is virtually impossible, when the traditional rule of law no longer provides consistent justice, when the economic system no longer produces wealth for the middle class, stripping them of their future, then what would you expect people to do? When they have been told the world is

dying because of global warming and its *their* fault, when parents
are repeatedly told that:

> *Too many people on the bus from the airport*
>
> *Too many holes in the crust of the earth*
>
> *The planet groans*
>
> *Every time it registers another birth*[242]

Biblical morality is a distant memory with the banning of prayer
in public schools and the removal of the Ten Commandments
from all civic institutions. Yet, these were the original guideposts
given to properly run our Constitutional Republic.

In short, people are disillusioned, disoriented, hopeless and
very angry. Worse, they have been left with no outlet to resolve
their anger, and unresolved anger invariably gives way to outright
rage.

Unfortunately, this is the state of society today, and no
amount of political wrangling will make one whit of difference.
The only way to restore law and order in America is to put the
Constitutional Republic back in place, electing leaders who will
actually obey their oath of office to "support and defend" it. As
discussed in the previous chapter, this is a long-shot from the top
down, but a real possibility from the bottom up.

Rockefeller: The Fountainhead

I have expended a lot of effort in an attempt to expose the
mind of Technocracy and its perpetrators. Unless you can "get inside their heads", you really cannot understand what makes them
tick. In that vein, there are two more things to say about the late
David Rockefeller who gave us the Trilateral Commission, and
Technocracy under the label of Sustainable Development. While
many viewed him as a benevolent philanthropist, they could not
have been farther from the truth.

---

242 United Nations, *Rescue Mission Planet Earth: A Children's Edition of Agenda 21*, 1994, p. 32.
(Original lyrics and song by Paul Simon, Born At The Right Time, 1990.)

The idea for the Trilateral Commission was originally conceived in 1972 at a Bilderberg meeting in Europe. It was founded the next year and Rockefeller invited several media giants (mostly those who were already attending Bilderberg meetings) into membership and then promptly gave them a gag order to *not report* whatever they would hear. (Yes, this was censorship back in 1973!) These included the head of CBS, *Chicago Sun-Times*, *Washington Post*, *Time Magazine*, Media General, Times-Mirror, *New York Times*, Corporation for Public Broadcasting, Dow Jones, *Wall Street Journal* and others.[243] Collectively, these were the power elite of the media world and what they would write about would determine what eventually got into the history books 25 years later. Their conspicuous silence was finally praised by Rockefeller himself when he addressed the 1991 Bilderberg gathering:

> *We are grateful to The Washington Post, The New York Times, Time Magazine and other great publications whose directors have attended our meetings and respected their promises of discretion for almost forty years. It would have been impossible for us to develop our plan for the world if we had been subject to the bright lights of publicity during those years. But, the work is now much more sophisticated and prepared to march towards a World Government. The supranational sovereignty of an intellectual elite and world bankers is surely preferable to the national auto-determination practiced in past centuries.[244]*

In short, Rockefeller despised the Western world and especially America's Constitutional Republic. Like a clever Indian in an old Tom Mix western, he methodically covered his tracks every inch of the way so that he could not be tracked. It is no wonder that the American people never figured out what was really happening behind the scenes. For all those who blew the whistle on their fraudulent schemes, like Antony Sutton and myself, we were

---

243 Sutton, Antony C. and Patrick M. Wood, *Trilaterals Over Washington, Vol. 1.*, [August Corporation, 1979], p. 37-38.
244 *Minutes, Lectures Francaises*, Hilaire du Berrier Report, July/August, 1991.

alternatively branded as the lunatic fringe on the right or the left, while always positioning Trilaterals in the moderate middle.

Ten years later at the age of 87, Rockefeller felt the need to write an auto-biography, which he called *Memoirs*. It was a rambling account of his life, places he went, stories about family, things he influenced, etc. It was also a blunt stick-a-finger-in-your-eye admission of his role in yanking America right out from under us:

> *Some even believe we [Rockefeller family] are part of a secret*
> *cabal working against the best interests of the United States,*
> *characterizing my family and me as 'internationalists' and of*
> *conspiring with others around the world to build a more in-*
> *tegrated global political and economic structure - One World,*
> *if you will. If that's the charge, I stand guilty, and I am proud*
> *of it.*[245]

Think back to the end of Chapter 6 and the story of Dr. William Livingston, aka William Avery Rockefeller, Sr. This was the great grandfather of David Rockefeller. Did the fruit fall far from the tree? Hardly. Both were lying deceivers, con men and hucksters. David only played his part with a lot more money at his disposal, with which he purchased legitimacy, stature and respect; otherwise, they are two peas in the same pod. Although character-equivalent, they had two different props: William sold a cancer cure consisting of oil and laxative; David promoted global economic domination in the name of Sustainable Development and environmentalism.

As to the rest of the myriad actors on the Rockefeller stage, consisting of multinational corporations, the Sustainable Development hucksters at the United Nations, hundreds of NGOs, politicians, lobbyists and radical environmentalists, it is no mystery why deception and fraud run amok: as the ancient proverb states, "The fish stinks from the head." With Rockefeller as the grand mentor, who would voluntarily choose to take the high road of honesty, ethics and morality?

---

245 David Rockefeller, *Memoirs*, [Random House, 2002], p. 406.

Lastly, I would point out that Rockefeller purposely misled with his "One World" comment. While it is definitely economic in nature because Technocracy and Sustainable Development are, in fact, an alternative economic system designed to replace Capitalism and Free Enterprise, hinting at a political structure is wrong. *Governance* does not necessarily imply *government*. A fully-managed economic system demands managerial control, but this can be done with advanced technology instead of politicians. This has been duly noted by experts like Dr. Parag Khanna, author of the globalist book, *Connectography*:

> *We are building the global society without a global leader. Global order is no longer something that can be dictated or controlled from the top down.* ***Globalization itself is the order.***[246] [emphasis added]

The Hard Road

Since 1973, America has indeed been placed on a hard road to world order. It was not our choice, but we have felt the wrenching transformation every step of the way. Our entire nation has been saturated with UN policies of Agenda 21, 2030 Agenda and New Urban Agenda, all of which are in support of destroying Capitalism and Free Enterprise for the sake of Sustainable Development and Technocracy.

Property rights have been drastically eroded. Income and wealth inequality has become exaggerated to the extreme while the middle class has all but vanished. Political institutions are dysfunctional and ineffective. The social culture has been radically transformed into one of anger, hatred and bitterness. Ignorance of history has left us as a nation without a past. Everything from our personal data to our traditional government institutions have been weaponized against us. Our American culture has converted to multi-culturalism with massive immigration. The traditional Rule of Law has been shredded. And on and on it goes. The America we have today is clearly not the America we had in

---

246 Khanna, Parag, Connectography: Mapping the Future of Global Civilization (Kindle Locations 528-530). Random House Publishing Group. Kindle Edition.

1973, and the downhill progression had nothing to do with natural evolution. An argument has been made that Humpty Dumpty (America) was already sitting on the wall back then, to which this writer responds, "Humpty was pushed."

The reader can judge for himself if Richard Gardner's *Hard Road to World Order* was accurate or not:

It will look like a great "booming, buzzing confusion," but an end-run around national sovereignty, eroding it piece by piece, will accomplish much more than the old-fashioned frontal assault.[247]

Final Thoughts

In America, the first line of defence against attacks on our Constitution is found in the First Amendment, which states,

Congress shall make no law respecting an establishment of religion, or prohibiting the free exercise thereof; or abridging the freedom of speech, or of the press; or the right of the people peaceably to assemble, and to petition the Government for a redress of grievances.

Each item mentioned here implies direct action: the *exercise* of religion, *speaking* your mind, *writing* words on a page, *assembling* together and *petitioning* the government. If you are not doing one or more of these, then it is just so much ink on a page. Those con artists who would completely destroy the Constitution know full well that it will fall like a house of cards if the First Amendment can be effectively nullified.

This is why we have been browbeaten into silence with political correctness, label lynching and fear. This is why censorship has been weaponized to squash freedom of the press. This is why those who would protest are excoriated and intimidated by threats of physical violence. This is why the channels for petitioning the government have been blockaded. All combined, these attacks have created a societal pressure cooker that is going to explode if we do not stand up to the attacks and reclaim the high

247   *Foreign Affairs, Vol. 52, Number 3, 1974, pp 557-576..*

ground of the First Amendment, but this cannot be done without action.

It was for this very reason that this writer established **Citizens for Free Speech** as a non-profit and tax-exempt organization to defend and support the First Amendment and to encourage local action consistent with its principles. Every American has these inherent rights if they would only stand up to exercise them. The marketplace of ideas is overwhelmed with a plethora of anti-American rhetoric: Socialism, Communism, Sustainable Development, label-lynching and everything in between. Is there any compelling reason that any of these should win the battle for the soul of America? This writer thinks not, and suggests that most Americans would agree.

There is no one to challenge us but ourselves, and if we fail to do so, we can be certain of the eventual outcome. You are welcome to join and participate with **Citizens for Free Speech** to make your voice heard.

www.CitizensForFreeSpeech.org

This page left intentionally blank

APPENDIX I

HABITAT III

NEW URBAN AGENDA

Draft outcome document for adoption in Quito

10 September 2016

QUITO DECLARATION ON SUSTAINABLE CITIES AND HUMAN SETTLEMENTS FOR ALL

1. We, the Heads of State and Government, Ministers and High Representatives, have gathered at the United Nations Conference on Housing and Sustainable Urban Development (Habitat III) from 17 to 20 October 2016 in Quito, Ecuador, with the participation of sub-national and local governments, parliamentarians, civil society, indigenous peoples and local communities, the private sector, professionals and practitioners, the scientific and academic community, and other relevant stakeholders, to adopt a New Urban Agenda.

2. By 2050 the world urban population is expected to nearly double, making urbanization one of the 21st century's most

transformative trends. As the population, economic activities, social and cultural interactions, as well as environmental and humanitarian impacts, are increasingly concentrated in cities, this poses massive sustainability challenges in terms of housing, infrastructure, basic services, food security, health, education, decent jobs, safety, and natural resources, among others.

3. Since the United Nations Conferences on Human Settlements in Vancouver in 1976 and in Istanbul in 1996, and the adoption of the Millennium Development Goals in 2000, we have seen improvements in the quality of life of millions of urban inhabitants, including slum and informal settlement dwellers. However, the persistence of multiple forms of poverty, growing inequalities, and environmental degradation, remain among the major obstacles to sustainable development worldwide, with social and economic exclusion and spatial segregation often an irrefutable reality in cities and human settlements.

4. We are still far from adequately addressing these and other existing and emerging challenges; and there is a need to take advantage of the opportunities of urbanization as an engine of sustained and inclusive economic growth, social and cultural development, and environmental protection, and of its potential contributions to the achievement of transformative and sustainable development.

5. By readdressing the way cities and human settlements are planned, designed, financed, developed, governed, and managed, the New Urban Agenda will help to end poverty and hunger in all its forms and dimensions, reduce inequalities, promote sustained, inclusive, and sustainable economic growth, achieve gender equality and the empowerment of all women and girls, in order to fully harness their vital contribution to sustainable development, improve human health and well-being, as well as foster resilience and protect the environment.

6. We take full account of the milestone achievements in the course of the year 2015, in particular the 2030 Agenda for Sustainable Development, including the Sustainable Development Goals (SDGs), and the Addis Ababa Action Agenda of the Third International Conference on Financing for Development, the Paris Agreement adopted under the United Nations Framework

Convention on Climate Change (UNFCC), the Sendai Framework for Disaster Risk Reduction 2015-2030, the Vienna Programme of Action for Landlocked Developing Countries for the Decade 2014-2024, the Small Island Developing States Accelerated Modalities of Action (SAMOA) Pathway and the Istanbul Programme of Action for the Least Developed Countries for the Decade 2011-2020. We also take account of the Rio Declaration on Environment and Development, the World Summit on Sustainable Development, the World Summit for Social Development, the International Conference on Population and Development Programme of Action, the Beijing Platform for Action, and the United Nations Conference on Sustainable Development, and the follow up to these conferences.

7. While recognizing that it did not have an intergovernmental agreed outcome, we take note of the World Humanitarian Summit in May 2016 in Istanbul.

8. We acknowledge the contributions of national governments, as well as the contributions of sub-national and local governments, in the definition of the New Urban Agenda and take note of the second World Assembly of Local and Regional Governments.

9. This New Urban Agenda reaffirms our global commitment to sustainable urban development as a critical step for realizing sustainable development in an integrated and coordinated manner at global, regional, national, sub-national, and local levels, with the participation of all relevant actors. The implementation of 2 the New Urban Agenda contributes to the implementation and localization of the 2030 Agenda for Sustainable Development in an integrated manner, and to the achievement of the Sustainable Development Goals (SDGs) and targets, including SDG 11 of making cities and human settlements inclusive, safe, resilient, and sustainable.

10. The New Urban Agenda acknowledges that culture and cultural diversity are sources of enrichment for humankind and provides an important contribution to the sustainable development of cities, human settlements, and citizens, empowering them to play an active and unique role in development initiatives; and further recognizes that culture should be taken into account in the promotion and implementation of new sustainable consumption

and production patterns that contribute to the responsible use of resources and address the adverse impact of climate change.

Our shared vision

11. We share a vision of cities for all, referring to the equal use and enjoyment of cities and human settlements, seeking to promote inclusivity and ensure that all inhabitants, of present and future generations, without discrimination of any kind, are able to inhabit and produce just, safe, healthy, accessible, affordable, resilient, and sustainable cities and human settlements, to foster prosperity and quality of life for all. We note the efforts of some national and local governments to enshrine this vision, referred to as right to the city, in their legislations, political declarations and charters.

12. We aim to achieve cities and human settlements where all persons are able to enjoy equal rights and opportunities, as well as their fundamental freedoms, guided by the purposes and principles of the Charter of the United Nations, including full respect for international law. In this regard, the New Urban Agenda is grounded in the Universal Declaration of Human Rights, international human rights treaties, the Millennium Declaration, and the 2005 World Summit Outcome. It is informed by other instruments such as the Declaration on the Right to Development.

13. We envisage cities and human settlements that:

(a) fulfill their social function, including the social and ecological function of land, with a view to progressively achieve the full realization of the right to adequate housing, as a component of the right to an adequate standard of living, without discrimination, universal access to safe and affordable drinking water and sanitation, as well as equal access for all to public goods and quality services in areas such as food security and nutrition, health, education, infrastructure, mobility and transportation, energy, air quality, and livelihoods;

(b) are participatory, promote civic engagement, engender a sense of belonging and ownership among all their inhabitants, prioritize safe, inclusive, accessible, green, and quality public spaces, friendly for families, enhance social and intergenerational interactions, cultural expressions, and political participation, as appropriate, and foster social cohesion, inclusion, and safety in peaceful and pluralistic societies, where the needs of all inhabitants are met, recognizing the specific needs of those in vulnerable situations;

(c) achieve gender equality and empower all women and girls, ensuring women's full and effective participation and equal rights in all fields and in leadership at all levels of decision-making, and by ensuring decent work and equal pay for equal work, or work of equal value for all women, as well as preventing and eliminating all forms of discrimination, violence, and harassment against women and girls in private and public spaces;

(d) meet the challenges and opportunities of present and future sustained, inclusive, and sustainable economic growth, leveraging urbanization for structural transformation, high productivity, valueadded activities, and resource efficiency, harnessing local economies, taking note of the contribution of the informal economy while supporting a sustainable transition to the formal economy;

(e) fulfill their territorial functions across administrative boundaries, and act as hubs and drivers for balanced sustainable and integrated urban and territorial development at all levels; 3

(f) promote age- and gender-responsive planning and investment for sustainable, safe, and accessible urban mobility for all and resource efficient transport systems for passengers and freight, effectively linking people, places, goods, services, and economic opportunities;

(g) adopt and implement disaster risk reduction and management, reduce vulnerability, build resilience and responsiveness to natural and man-made hazards, and foster mitigation and adaptation to climate change;

(h) protect, conserve, restore, and promote their ecosystems, water, natural habitats, and biodiversity, minimize their environmental impact, and change to sustainable consumption and production patterns.

Our Principles and Commitments

14. To achieve our vision, we resolve to adopt a New Urban Agenda guided by the following interlinked principles:

(a) Leave no one behind, by ending poverty in all its forms and dimensions, including the eradication of extreme poverty, by ensuring equal rights and opportunities, socio-economic and cultural diversity, integration in the urban space, enhancing liveability, education, food security and nutrition, health and well-being; including by ending the epidemics of AIDS, tuberculosis, and malaria, promoting safety and eliminating discrimination and all forms of violence; ensuring public participation providing safe and equal access for all; and providing equal access for all to physical and social infrastructure and basic services as well as adequate and affordable housing.

(b) Sustainable and inclusive urban economies, by leveraging the agglomeration benefits of well-planned urbanization, high productivity, competitiveness, and innovation; promoting full and productive employment and decent work for all, ensuring decent job creation and equal access for all to economic and productive resources and opportunities; preventing land speculation; and promoting secure land tenure and managing urban shrinking where appropriate.

(c) Environmental sustainability, by promoting clean energy, sustainable use of land and resources in urban development as well as protecting ecosystems and biodiversity, including adopting healthy lifestyles in harmony with nature; promoting sustainable consumption and production patterns; building urban resilience; reducing disaster risks; and mitigating and adapting to climate change.

15. We commit to work towards an urban paradigm shift for a New Urban Agenda that will:

(a) readdress the way we plan, finance, develop, govern, and manage cities and human settlements, recognizing sustainable urban and territorial development as essential to the achievement of sustainable development and prosperity for all;

(b) recognize the leading role of national governments, as appropriate, in the definition and implementation of inclusive and effective urban policies and legislation for sustainable urban development, and the equally important contributions of sub-national and local governments, as well as civil society and other relevant stakeholders, in a transparent and accountable manner;

(c) adopt sustainable, people-centered, age- and gender-responsive and integrated approaches to urban and territorial development by implementing policies, strategies, capacity development, and actions at all levels, based on fundamental drivers of change including:

i. developing and implementing urban policies at the appropriate level including within local-national and multi-stakeholder partnerships, building integrated systems of cities and human settlements, promoting cooperation among all levels of government to enable them to achieve sustainable integrated urban development;

ii. strengthening urban governance, with sound institutions and mechanisms that empower and include urban stakeholders, as well as appropriate checks and balances, providing predictability and coherence in the urban development plans to enable social 4 inclusion, sustained, inclusive, and sustainable economic growth and environmental protection;

iii. reinvigorating long-term and integrated urban and territorial planning and design in order to optimize the spatial dimension of the urban form and to deliver the positive outcomes of urbanization;

iv. supporting effective, innovative, and sustainable financing frameworks and instruments, enabling strengthened municipal finance and local fiscal systems in order to create, sustain, and share the value generated by sustainable urban development in an inclusive manner.

Call for Action

16. While the specific circumstances of cities of all sizes, towns, and villages vary, we affirm that the New Urban Agenda is universal in scope, participatory, and people-centered, protects the planet, and has a long-term vision, setting out priorities and actions at the global, regional, national, sub-national, and local levels that governments and other relevant stakeholders in every country can adopt based on

their needs.

17. We will work to implement this New Urban Agenda within our own countries and at the regional and global levels, taking into account different national realities, capacities, and levels of development, and respecting national legislations and practices, as well as policies and priorities.

18. We reaffirm all of the principles of the Rio Declaration on Environment and Development, including, inter alia, the principle of common but differentiated responsibilities, as set out in Principle 7 thereof.

19. We acknowledge that in implementing the New Urban Agenda, particular attention should be given to addressing the unique and emerging urban development challenges facing all countries, in particular developing countries, including African countries, least developed countries, landlocked developing countries, and small-island developing States, as well as the specific challenges facing the middle income countries. Special attention should also be given to countries in situations of conflicts, as well as countries and territories under foreign occupation, post-conflict countries, and countries affected by natural and manmade disasters.

20. We recognize the need to give particular attention to addressing multiple forms of discrimination faced by, inter alia, women and girls, children and youth, persons with disabilities, people living with HIV/AIDS, older persons, indigenous peoples and local communities, slum and informal settlement dwellers, homeless people, workers, smallholder farmers and fishers, refugees, returnees and internally displaced persons, and migrants, regardless of migration status.

21. We urge all national, sub-national, and local governments, as well as all relevant stakeholders, in line with national policies and legislation, to revitalize, strengthen, and create partnerships, enhancing coordination and cooperation to effectively implement the New Urban Agenda and realize our shared vision.

22. We adopt this New Urban Agenda as a collective vision and a political commitment to promote and realize sustainable urban development, and as a historic opportunity to leverage the key role of cities and human settlements as drivers of sustainable development in an increasingly urbanized world.

23. We resolve to implement the New Urban Agenda as a key instrument for national, sub-national, and local governments and all relevant stakeholders to achieve sustainable urban development.[241]

---

241 There are a total of 175 numbered paragraphs in this document. The full document can be downloaded https://www.Technocracy. News/New-Urban-Agenda

SUSTAINABLE DEVELOPMENT GOALS

GENERAL ASSEMBLY

Transforming our world: the 2030 Agenda for Sustainable Development

September 2015

Goal 1. End poverty in all its forms everywhere

1.1 By 2030, eradicate extreme poverty for all people everywhere, currently measured as people living on less than $1.25 a day

1.2 By 2030, reduce at least by half the proportion of men, women and children of all ages living in poverty in all its dimensions according to national definitions

1.3 Implement nationally appropriate social protection systems and measures for all, including floors, and by 2030 achieve substantial coverage of the poor and the vulnerable

1.4 By 2030, ensure that all men and women, in particular the poor and the vulnerable, have equal rights to economic resources, as well as access to basic services, ownership and control over land and other forms of property, inheritance, natural resources, appropriate new technology and financial services, including microfinance

1.5 By 2030, build the resilience of the poor and those in vulnerable situations and reduce their exposure and vulnerability to climate-related extreme events and other economic, social and environmental shocks and disasters

1.a   Ensure significant mobilization of resources from a variety of sources, including through enhanced development cooperation, in order to provide adequate and predictable means for developing countries, in particular least developed countries, to implement programmes and policies to end poverty in all its dimensions

1.b   Create sound policy frameworks at the national, regional and international levels, based on pro-poor and gender-sensitive development strategies, to support accelerated investment in poverty eradication actions

Goal 2. End hunger, achieve food security and improved nutrition and promote sustainable agriculture

2.1   By 2030, end hunger and ensure access by all people, in particular the poor and people in vulnerable situations, including infants, to safe, nutritious and sufficient food all year round

2.2   By 2030, end all forms of malnutrition, including achieving, by 2025, the internationally agreed targets on stunting and wasting in children under 5 years of age, and address the nutritional needs of adolescent girls, pregnant and lactating women and older persons

2.3   By 2030, double the agricultural productivity and incomes of small-scale food producers, in particular women, indigenous peoples, family farmers, pastoralists and fishers, including through secure and equal access to land, other productive resources and inputs, knowledge, financial services, markets and opportunities for value addition and non-farm employment

2.4   By 2030, ensure sustainable food production systems and implement resilient agricultural practices that increase productivity and production, that help maintain ecosystems, that strengthen capacity for adaptation to climate change, extreme weather, drought, flooding and other disasters and that progressively improve land and soil quality

2.5   By 2020, maintain the genetic diversity of seeds, cultivated plants and farmed and domesticated animals and their related wild species, including through soundly managed and diversified seed and plant banks at the national, regional and international levels, and promote access to and fair and equitable sharing of benefits arising from the utilization of genetic resources and associated traditional knowledge, as internationally agreed

2.a   Increase investment, including through enhanced international cooperation, in rural infrastructure, agricultural research and extension services, technology development and plant and livestock gene banks in order to enhance agricultural productive capacity in developing countries, in particular least developed countries

2.b   Correct and prevent trade restrictions and distortions in world agricultural markets, including through the parallel elimination of all forms of agricultural export subsidies and all export measures with equivalent effect, in accordance with the mandate of the Doha Development Round

2.c   Adopt measures to ensure the proper functioning of food commodity markets and their derivatives and facilitate timely access to market information, including on food reserves, in order to help limit extreme food price volatility

Goal 3. Ensure healthy lives and promote well-being for all at all ages

3.1   By 2030, reduce the global maternal mortality ratio to less than 70 per 100,000 live births

3.2   By 2030, end preventable deaths of newborns and children under 5 years of age, with all countries aiming to reduce neonatal mortality to at least as low as 12 per 1,000 live births and under 5 mortality to at least as low as 25 per 1,000 live births

3.3   By 2030, end the epidemics of AIDS, tuberculosis, malaria and neglected tropical diseases and combat hepatitis, waterborne diseases and other communicable diseases

3.4   By 2030, reduce by one third premature mortality from non-communicable diseases through prevention and treatment and promote mental health and well-being

3.5 Strengthen the prevention and treatment of substance abuse, including narcotic drug abuse and harmful use of alcohol

3.6 By 2020, halve the number of global deaths and injuries from road traffic accidents

3.7 By 2030, ensure universal access to sexual and reproductive health-care services, including for family planning, information and education, and the integration of reproductive health into national strategies and programmes

3.8 Achieve universal health coverage, including financial risk protection, access to quality essential health-care services and access to safe, effective, quality and affordable essential medicines and vaccines for all

3.9 By 2030, substantially reduce the number of deaths and illnesses from hazardous chemicals and air, water and soil pollution and contamination

3.a Strengthen the implementation of the World Health Organization Framework Convention on Tobacco Control in all countries, as appropriate

3.b Support the research and development of vaccines and medicines for the communicable and non-communicable diseases that primarily affect developing countries, provide access to affordable essential medicines and vaccines, in accordance with the Doha Declaration on the TRIPS Agreement and Public Health, which affirms the right of developing countries to use to the full the provisions in the Agreement on Trade-Related Aspects of Intellectual Property Rights regarding flexibilities to protect public health, and, in particular, provide access to medicines for all

3.c Substantially increase health financing and the recruitment, development, training and retention of the health workforce in developing countries, especially in least developed countries and small island developing States

3.d Strengthen the capacity of all countries, in particular developing countries, for early warning, risk reduction and management of national and global health risks

Goal 4. Ensure inclusive and equitable quality education and promote lifelong learning op-

portunities for all

4.1   By 2030, ensure that all girls and boys complete free, equitable and quality primary and secondary education leading to relevant and effective learning outcomes

4.2   By 2030, ensure that all girls and boys have access to quality early childhood development, care and pre-primary education so that they are ready for primary education

4.3   By 2030, ensure equal access for all women and men to affordable and quality technical, vocational and tertiary education, including university

4.4   By 2030, substantially increase the number of youth and adults who have relevant skills, including technical and vocational skills, for employment, decent jobs and entrepreneurship

4.5   By 2030, eliminate gender disparities in education and ensure equal access to all levels of education and vocational training for the vulnerable, including persons with disabilities, indigenous peoples and children in vulnerable situations

4.6   By 2030, ensure that all youth and a substantial proportion of adults, both men and women, achieve literacy and numeracy

4.7   By 2030, ensure that all learners acquire the knowledge and skills needed to promote sustainable development, including, among others, through education for sustainable development and sustainable lifestyles, human rights, gender equality, promotion of a culture of peace and non-violence, global citizenship and appreciation of cultural diversity and of culture's contribution to sustainable development

4.a   Build and upgrade education facilities that are child, disability and gender sensitive and provide safe, non-violent, inclusive and effective learning environments for all

4.b   By 2020, substantially expand globally the number of scholarships available to developing countries, in particular least developed countries, small island developing States and African countries, for enrolment in higher education, including vocational training and information and communications technology, technical, engineering and scientific programmes, in developed countries and other developing countries

4.c By 2030, substantially increase the supply of qualified teachers, including through international cooperation for teacher training in developing countries, especially least developed countries and small island developing States

Goal 5. Achieve gender equality and empower all women and girls

5.1 End all forms of discrimination against all women and girls everywhere

5.2 Eliminate all forms of violence against all women and girls in the public and private spheres, including trafficking and sexual and other types of exploitation

5.3 Eliminate all harmful practices, such as child, early and forced marriage and female genital mutilation

5.4 Recognize and value unpaid care and domestic work through the provision of public services, infrastructure and social protection policies and the promotion of shared responsibility within the household and the family as nationally appropriate

5.5 Ensure women's full and effective participation and equal opportunities for leadership at all levels of decision-making in political, economic and public life

5.6 Ensure universal access to sexual and reproductive health and reproductive rights as agreed in accordance with the Programme of Action of the International Conference on Population and Development and the Beijing Platform for Action and the outcome documents of their review conferences

5.a Undertake reforms to give women equal rights to economic resources, as well as access to ownership and control over land and other forms of property, financial services, inheritance and natural resources, in accordance with national laws

5.b Enhance the use of enabling technology, in particular information and communications technology, to promote the empowerment of women

5.c Adopt and strengthen sound policies and enforceable legislation for the promotion of gender equality and the empowerment of all women and girls at all levels

Goal 6. Ensure availability and sustainable management of water and sanitation for all

6.1 By 2030, achieve universal and equitable access to safe and affordable drinking water for all

6.2 By 2030, achieve access to adequate and equitable sanitation and hygiene for all and end open defecation, paying special attention to the needs of women and girls and those in vulnerable situations

6.3 By 2030, improve water quality by reducing pollution, eliminating dumping and minimizing release of hazardous chemicals and materials, halving the proportion of untreated wastewater and substantially increasing recycling and safe reuse globally

6.4 By 2030, substantially increase water-use efficiency across all sectors and ensure sustainable withdrawals and supply of freshwater to address water scarcity and substantially reduce the number of people suffering from water scarcity

6.5 By 2030, implement integrated water resources management at all levels, including through transboundary cooperation as appropriate

6.6 By 2020, protect and restore water-related ecosystems, including mountains, forests, wetlands, rivers, aquifers and lakes

6.a By 2030, expand international cooperation and capacity-building support to developing countries in water- and sanitation-related activities and programmes, including water harvesting, desalination, water efficiency, wastewater treatment, recycling and reuse technologies

6.b Support and strengthen the participation of local communities in improving water and sanitation management

Goal 7. Ensure access to affordable, reliable, sustainable and modern energy for all

7.1 By 2030, ensure universal access to affordable, reliable and modern energy services

7.2 By 2030, increase substantially the share of renewable energy in the global energy mix

7.3   By 2030, double the global rate of improvement in energy efficiency

7.a   By 2030, enhance international cooperation to facilitate access to clean energy research and technology, including renewable energy, energy efficiency and advanced and cleaner fossil-fuel technology, and promote investment in energy infrastructure and clean energy technology

7.b   By 2030, expand infrastructure and upgrade technology for supplying modern and sustainable energy services for all in developing countries, in particular least developed countries, small island developing States and landlocked developing countries, in accordance with their respective programmes of support

Goal 8. Promote sustained, inclusive and sustainable economic growth, full and productive employment and decent work for all

8.1   Sustain per capita economic growth in accordance with national circumstances and, in particular, at least 7 per cent gross domestic product growth per annum in the least developed countries

8.2   Achieve higher levels of economic productivity through diversification, technological upgrading and innovation, including through a focus on high-value added and labour-intensive sectors

8.3   Promote development-oriented policies that support productive activities, decent job creation, entrepreneurship, creativity and innovation, and encourage the formalization and growth of micro-, small- and medium-sized enterprises, including through access to financial services

8.4   Improve progressively, through 2030, global resource efficiency in consumption and production and endeavour to decouple economic growth from environmental degradation, in accordance with the 10 Year Framework of Programmes on Sustainable Consumption and Production, with developed countries taking the lead

8.5   By 2030, achieve full and productive employment and decent work for all women and men, including for young people and persons with disabilities, and equal pay for work of equal value

8.6   By 2020, substantially reduce the proportion of youth not in employment, education or training

8.7   Take immediate and effective measures to eradicate forced labour, end modern slavery and human trafficking and secure the prohibition and elimination of the worst forms of child labour, including recruitment and use of child soldiers, and by 2025 end child labour in all its forms

8.8   Protect labour rights and promote safe and secure working environments for all workers, including migrant workers, in particular women migrants, and those in precarious employment

8.9   By 2030, devise and implement policies to promote sustainable tourism that creates jobs and promotes local culture and products

8.10 Strengthen the capacity of domestic financial institutions to encourage and expand access to banking, insurance and financial services for all

8.a   Increase Aid for Trade support for developing countries, in particular least developed countries, including through the Enhanced Integrated Framework for Trade-related Technical Assistance to Least Developed Countries

8.b   By 2020, develop and operationalize a global strategy for youth employment and implement the Global Jobs Pact of the International Labour Organization

Goal 9. Build resilient infrastructure, promote inclusive and sustainable industrialization and foster innovation

9.1   Develop quality, reliable, sustainable and resilient infrastructure, including regional and transborder infrastructure, to support economic development and human well-being, with a focus on affordable and equitable access for all

9.2   Promote inclusive and sustainable industrialization and, by 2030, significantly raise industry's share of employment and gross domestic product, in line with national circumstances, and double its share in least developed countries

9.3 Increase the access of small-scale industrial and other enterprises, in particular in developing countries, to financial services, including affordable credit, and their integration into value chains and markets

9.4 By 2030, upgrade infrastructure and retrofit industries to make them sustainable, with increased resource-use efficiency and greater adoption of clean and environmentally sound technologies and industrial processes, with all countries taking action in accordance with their respective capabilities

9.5 Enhance scientific research, upgrade the technological capabilities of industrial sectors in all countries, in particular developing countries, including, by 2030, encouraging innovation and substantially increasing the number of research and development workers per 1 million people and public and private research and development spending

9.a Facilitate sustainable and resilient infrastructure development in developing countries through enhanced financial, technological and technical support to African countries, least developed countries, landlocked developing countries and small island developing States

9.b Support domestic technology development, research and innovation in developing countries, including by ensuring a conducive policy environment for, inter alia, industrial diversification and value addition to commodities

9.c Significantly increase access to information and communications technology and strive to provide universal and affordable access to the Internet in least developed countries by 2020

Goal 10. Reduce inequality within and among countries

10.1 By 2030, progressively achieve and sustain income growth of the bottom 40 per cent of the population at a rate higher than the national average

10.2 By 2030, empower and promote the social, economic and political inclusion of all, irrespective of age, sex, disability, race, ethnicity, origin, religion or economic or other status

10.3 Ensure equal opportunity and reduce inequalities of out-come, including by eliminating discriminatory laws, policies and practices and promoting appropriate legislation, policies and action in this regard

10.4 Adopt policies, especially fiscal, wage and social protection policies, and progressively achieve greater equality

10.5 Improve the regulation and monitoring of global financial markets and institutions and strengthen the implementation of such regulations

10.6 Ensure enhanced representation and voice for developing countries in decision-making in global international economic and financial institutions in order to deliver more effective, credible, accountable and legitimate institutions

10.7 Facilitate orderly, safe, regular and responsible migration and mobility of people, including through the implementation of planned and well-managed migration policies

10.a Implement the principle of special and differential treatment for developing countries, in particular least developed countries, in accordance with World Trade Organization agreements

10.b Encourage official development assistance and financial flows, including foreign direct investment, to States where the need is greatest, in particular least developed countries, African countries, small island developing States and landlocked developing countries, in accordance with their national plans and programmes

10.c By 2030, reduce to less than 3 per cent the transaction costs of migrant remittances and eliminate remittance corridors with costs higher than 5 per cent

Goal 11. Make cities and human settlements inclusive, safe, resilient and sustainable

11.1 By 2030, ensure access for all to adequate, safe and affordable housing and basic services and upgrade slums

11.2 By 2030, provide access to safe, affordable, accessible and sustainable transport systems for all, improving road safety, notably by expanding public transport, with special attention to the needs of those in vulnerable situations, women, children, persons with disabilities and older persons

11.3 By 2030, enhance inclusive and sustainable urbanization and capacity for participatory, integrated and sustainable human settlement planning and management in all countries

11.4 Strengthen efforts to protect and safeguard the world's cultural and natural heritage

11.5 By 2030, significantly reduce the number of deaths and the number of people affected and substantially decrease the direct economic losses relative to global gross domestic product caused by disasters, including water-related disasters, with a focus on protecting the poor and people in vulnerable situations

11.6 By 2030, reduce the adverse per capita environmental impact of cities, including by paying special attention to air quality and municipal and other waste management

11.7 By 2030, provide universal access to safe, inclusive and accessible, green and public spaces, in particular for women and children, older persons and persons with disabilities

11.a Support positive economic, social and environmental links between urban, peri-urban and rural areas by strengthening national and regional development planning

11.b By 2020, substantially increase the number of cities and human settlements adopting and implementing integrated policies and plans towards inclusion, resource efficiency, mitigation and adaptation to climate change, resilience to disasters, and develop and implement, in line with the Sendai Framework for Disaster Risk Reduction 2015–2030, holistic disaster risk management at all levels

11.c Support least developed countries, including through financial and technical assistance, in building sustainable and resilient buildings utilizing local materials

Goal 12. Ensure sustainable consumption and production patterns

12.1 Implement the 10 Year Framework of Programmes on Sustainable Consumption and Production Patterns, all countries taking action, with developed countries taking the lead, taking into account the development and capabilities of developing countries

12.2 By 2030, achieve the sustainable management and efficient use of natural resources

12.3 By 2030, halve per capita global food waste at the retail and consumer levels and reduce food losses along production and supply chains, including post-harvest losses

12.4 By 2020, achieve the environmentally sound management of chemicals and all wastes throughout their life cycle, in accordance with agreed international frameworks, and significantly reduce their release to air, water and soil in order to minimize their adverse impacts on human health and the environment

12.5 By 2030, substantially reduce waste generation through prevention, reduction, recycling and reuse

12.6 Encourage companies, especially large and transnational companies, to adopt sustainable practices and to integrate sustainability information into their reporting cycle

12.7 Promote public procurement practices that are sustainable, in accordance with national policies and priorities

12.8 By 2030, ensure that people everywhere have the relevant information and awareness for sustainable development and lifestyles in harmony with nature

12.a Support developing countries to strengthen their scientific and technological capacity to move towards more sustainable patterns of consumption and production

12.b Develop and implement tools to monitor sustainable development impacts for sustainable tourism that creates jobs and promotes local culture and products

12.c Rationalize inefficient fossil-fuel subsidies that encourage wasteful consumption by removing market distortions, in accordance with national circumstances, including by restructuring taxation and phasing out those harmful subsidies, where they exist, to reflect their environmental impacts, taking fully into account the specific needs and conditions of developing countries and minimizing the possible adverse impacts on their development in a manner that protects the poor and the affected communities

* Acknowledging that the United Nations Framework Convention on Climate Change is the primary international, intergovernmental forum for negotiating the global response to climate change.

Goal 13. Take urgent action to combat climate change and its impacts*

13.1 Strengthen resilience and adaptive capacity to climate-related hazards and natural disasters in all countries

13.2 Integrate climate change measures into national policies, strategies and planning

13.3 Improve education, awareness-raising and human and institutional capacity on climate change mitigation, adaptation, impact reduction and early warning

13.a Implement the commitment undertaken by developed-country parties to the United Nations Framework Convention on Climate Change to a goal of mobilizing jointly $100 billion annually by 2020 from all sources to address the needs of developing countries in the context of meaningful mitigation actions and transparency on implementation and fully operationalize the Green Climate Fund through its capitalization as soon as possible

13.b Promote mechanisms for raising capacity for effective climate change-related planning and management in least developed countries and small island developing States, including focusing on women, youth and local and marginalized communities

Goal 14. Conserve and sustainably use the oceans, seas and marine resources for sustainable development

14.1 By 2025, prevent and significantly reduce marine pollution of all kinds, in particular from land-based activities, including marine debris and nutrient pollution

14.2 By 2020, sustainably manage and protect marine and

coastal ecosystems to avoid significant adverse impacts, including by strengthening their resilience, and take action for their restoration in order to achieve healthy and productive oceans

14.3 Minimize and address the impacts of ocean acidification, including through enhanced scientific cooperation at all levels

14.4 By 2020, effectively regulate harvesting and end overfishing, illegal, unreported and unregulated fishing and destructive fishing practices and implement science-based management plans, in order to restore fish stocks in the shortest time feasible, at least to levels that can produce maximum sustainable yield as determined by their biological characteristics

14.5 By 2020, conserve at least 10 per cent of coastal and marine areas, consistent with national and international law and based on the best available scientific information

14.6 By 2020, prohibit certain forms of fisheries subsidies which contribute to overcapacity and overfishing, eliminate subsidies that contribute to illegal, unreported and unregulated fishing and refrain from introducing new such subsidies, recognizing that appropriate and effective special and differential treatment for developing and least developed countries should be an integral part of the World Trade Organization fisheries subsidies negotiation

14.7 By 2030, increase the economic benefits to small island developing States and least developed countries from the sustainable use of marine resources, including through sustainable management of fisheries, aquaculture and tourism

14.a Increase scientific knowledge, develop research capacity and transfer marine technology, taking into account the Intergovernmental Oceanographic Commission Criteria and Guidelines on the Transfer of Marine Technology, in order to improve ocean health and to enhance the contribution of marine biodiversity to the development of developing countries, in particular small island developing States and least developed countries

14.b Provide access for small-scale artisanal fishers to marine resources and markets

14.c Enhance the conservation and sustainable use of oceans

and their resources by implementing international law as reflected in the United Nations Convention on the Law of the Sea, which provides the legal framework for the conservation and sustainable use of oceans and their resources, as recalled in paragraph 158 of "The future we want"

Goal 15. Protect, restore and promote sustainable use of terrestrial ecosystems, sustainably manage forests, combat desertification, and halt and reverse land degradation and halt biodiversity loss

15.1 By 2020, ensure the conservation, restoration and sustainable use of terrestrial and inland freshwater ecosystems and their services, in particular forests, wetlands, mountains and drylands, in line with obligations under international agreements

15.2 By 2020, promote the implementation of sustainable management of all types of forests, halt deforestation, restore degraded forests and substantially increase afforestation and reforestation globally

15.3 By 2030, combat desertification, restore degraded land and soil, including land affected by desertification, drought and floods, and strive to achieve a land degradation-neutral world

15.4 By 2030, ensure the conservation of mountain ecosystems, including their biodiversity, in order to enhance their capacity to provide benefits that are essential for sustainable development

15.5 Take urgent and significant action to reduce the degradation of natural habitats, halt the loss of biodiversity and, by 2020, protect and prevent the extinction of threatened species

15.6 Promote fair and equitable sharing of the benefits arising from the utilization of genetic resources and promote appropriate access to such resources, as internationally agreed

15.7 Take urgent action to end poaching and trafficking of protected species of flora and fauna and address both demand and supply of illegal wildlife products

15.8 By 2020, introduce measures to prevent the introduction and significantly reduce the impact of invasive alien species on land and water ecosystems and control or eradicate the priority species

15.9 By 2020, integrate ecosystem and biodiversity values into national and local planning, development processes, poverty reduction strategies and accounts

15.a Mobilize and significantly increase financial resources from all sources to conserve and sustainably use biodiversity and ecosystems

15.b Mobilize significant resources from all sources and at all levels to finance sustainable forest management and provide adequate incentives to developing countries to advance such management, including for conservation and reforestation

15.c Enhance global support for efforts to combat poaching and trafficking of protected species, including by increasing the capacity of local communities to pursue sustainable livelihood opportunities

Goal 16. Promote peaceful and inclusive societies for sustainable development, provide access to justice for all and build effective, accountable and inclusive institutions at all levels

16.1 Significantly reduce all forms of violence and related death rates everywhere

16.2 End abuse, exploitation, trafficking and all forms of violence against and torture of children

16.3 Promote the rule of law at the national and international levels and ensure equal access to justice for all

16.4 By 2030, significantly reduce illicit financial and arms flows, strengthen the recovery and return of stolen assets and combat all forms of organized crime

16.5 Substantially reduce corruption and bribery in all their forms

16.6 Develop effective, accountable and transparent institutions at all levels

16.7 Ensure responsive, inclusive, participatory and representative decision-making at all levels

16.8 Broaden and strengthen the participation of developing countries in the institutions of global governance

16.9 By 2030, provide legal identity for all, including birth registration

16.10   Ensure public access to information and protect fundamental freedoms, in accordance with national legislation and international agreements

16.a Strengthen relevant national institutions, including through international cooperation, for building capacity at all levels, in particular in developing countries, to prevent violence and combat terrorism and crime

16.b Promote and enforce non-discriminatory laws and policies for sustainable development

Goal 17. Strengthen the means of implementation and revitalize the Global Partnership for Sustainable Development

Finance

17.1 Strengthen domestic resource mobilization, including through international support to developing countries, to improve domestic capacity for tax and other revenue collection

17.2 Developed countries to implement fully their official development assistance commitments, including the commitment by many developed countries to achieve the target of 0.7 per cent of gross national income for official development assistance (ODA/GNI) to developing countries and 0.15 to 0.20 per cent of ODA/GNI to least developed countries; ODA providers are encouraged to consider setting a target to provide at least 0.20 per cent of ODA/GNI to least developed countries

17.3 Mobilize additional financial resources for developing countries from multiple sources

17.4 Assist developing countries in attaining long-term debt sustainability through coordinated policies aimed at fostering debt financing, debt relief and debt restructuring, as appropriate, and address the external debt of highly indebted poor countries to reduce debt distress

17.5 Adopt and implement investment promotion regimes for least developed countries

Technology

17.6 Enhance North-South, South-South and triangular regional and international cooperation on and access to science, technology and innovation and enhance knowledge sharing on mutually agreed terms, including through improved coordination among existing mechanisms, in particular at the United Nations level, and through a global technology facilitation mechanism

17.7 Promote the development, transfer, dissemination and diffusion of environmentally sound technologies to developing countries on favourable terms, including on concessional and preferential terms, as mutually agreed

17.8 Fully operationalize the technology bank and science, technology and innovation capacity-building mechanism for least developed countries by 2017 and enhance the use of enabling technology, in particular information and communications technology

Capacity-building

17.9 Enhance international support for implementing effective and targeted capacity-building in developing countries to support national plans to implement all the Sustainable Development Goals, including through North-South, South-South and triangular cooperation

Trade

17.10 Promote a universal, rules-based, open, non-discriminatory and equitable multilateral trading system under the World Trade Organization, including through the conclusion of negotiations under its Doha Development Agenda

17.11 Significantly increase the exports of developing countries, in particular with a view to doubling the least developed countries' share of global exports by 2020

17.12 Realize timely implementation of duty-free and quo-ta-free market access on a lasting basis for all least developed countries, consistent with World Trade Organization decisions, including by ensuring that preferential rules of origin applicable to imports from least developed countries are transparent and simple, and contribute to facilitating market access

Systemic issues

Policy and institutional coherence

17.13 Enhance global macroeconomic stability, including through policy coordination and policy coherence

17.14 Enhance policy coherence for sustainable development

17.15 Respect each country's policy space and leadership to establish and implement policies for poverty eradication and sustainable development

Multi-stakeholder partnerships

17.16 Enhance the Global Partnership for Sustainable Development, complemented by multi-stakeholder partnerships that mobilize and share knowledge, expertise, technology and financial resources, to support the achievement of the Sustainable Development Goals in all countries, in particular developing countries

17.17 Encourage and promote effective public, public-private and civil society partnerships, building on the experience and re-sourcing strategies of partnerships

Data, monitoring and accountability

17.18 By 2020, enhance capacity-building support to develop-ing countries, including for least developed countries and small island developing States, to increase significantly the availability of high-quality, timely and reliable data disaggregated by income, gender, age, race, ethnicity, migratory status, disability, geographic location and other characteristics relevant in national contexts

17.19 By 2030, build on existing initiatives to develop measurements of progress on sustainable development that complement gross domestic product, and support statistical capacity-building in developing countries

INDEX

Global Institute for Green Growth 61
Global Warming 12, 15
Google 142
Gore, Al 20, 79, 80, 94, 150
Greater Phoenix Economic Council 68
Greater Phoenix Smart Region Initiative 97–99
Green Deen 146
Green Economy 32, 116–117, 146
GreenFaith 145
Greenfield, Adam 63

H

Habitat II 47
Habitat III. *See* United Nations Conference on Housing and Sustainable Urban Development
Hard Road To World Order, The 2
Harvey, Larry 142
Hearst Communications 7
Hearst, Randolph 7–9, 15
Heck, Charles 149
High-Level Panel of Eminent Persons 34
High-Level Political Forum on Sustainable Development 34
Hitachi 58, 67
Hoover Institution 64
Houston, Drew 143
Huawei 58
Hubbert, M. King 9
Hubbert, Randolph 9–10
Humanism 136
HushMail 156
Huxley, Aldous 15, 101, 160

I

IBM 58
ICLEI 51–53
IEEE 67
Infrastructure 43, 72
Instagram 156
Interfaith Summit on Climate Change 145

International Council for Local Environmental Initiatives. *See* ICLEI
International Monetary Fund 76
International New Town Institute 61
International Social Transformation Conference 23
International trade 32
International Youth Environment and Development Network 21
Internet of Everything 129
Internet of Things 59, 68, 79, 129, 150
IoT. *See* Internet of Things
Islam 115–117

J

Jinping, Xi 74
John Hopkins 132
Judeo/Christian ethic 140
Jupiter 135

K

Khanna, Dr. Parag 3, 53, 77
Ki-moon, Ban 34–35
King, Larry 149
Kissinger, Henry 74
Knightscope 127
Kyoto Protocol 35

L

Laudato si 145
Levandowski, Anthony 143
Levingston, William 55–56
Lex Mercatoria 88
Litecoin 104
Livingston, William 168
LocalActivist 157
Local Governments for Sustainability. *See* ICLEI

M

Malaysia 116
Marduk 136

S

T

U

OTHER BOOKS BY PATRICK M. WOOD

Trilaterals Over Washington, Volumes I and II (Patrick Wood and Antony C. Sutton, 1978-80, Reprinted 2017)

Technocracy Rising: The Trojan Horse of Global Transformation (2015)

Globalization and the Crucible of Global Banking (2018)

For more information and current events on Technocracy, see:

WWW.TECHNOCRACY.NEWS

Coherent Publishing
P.O. Box 52247
Mesa, AZ 85247
Editor@Technocracy.News

Printed in Great Britain
by Amazon

71393922R00132